THE GREAT CASTLE HOTELS OF EUROPE

THE GREAT CASTLE HOTELS OF EUROPE

Phil Philcox & Beverly Boe

Photo reproduction: Robert Russell

ICARUS PRESS
South Bend, Indiana
1983

The Great Castle Hotels of Europe
Copyright © 1983 by Phil Philcox & Beverly Boe

1   2   3   4   5   6   87   86   85   84   83

Icarus Press, Inc.
Post Office Box 1225
South Bend, Indiana 46624

Library of Congress Cataloging in Publication Data

Philcox, Phil.
   The great castle hotels of Europe.

   Includes index.
    1. Hotels, taverns, etc. — Europe — Directories.
I. Boe, Beverly. II. Title.
TX910.A1P44   1983   647'.94401   82-23208
ISBN 0-89651-268-1

Dedication

To Ethel Webster, a mother to us both, who would have enjoyed experiencing these castle hotels

CONTENTS

ACKNOWLEDGMENTS

COMPILING A GUIDE TO THE GREAT CASTLES AND HISTORIC HOTELS OF Europe requires much more than just going there to collect information, photographs, and special experiences. We'd like to thank all of the contributors to this research-writing project for their information, photographs, tips, clues, suggestions, expertise and for sharing their special experiences. Without their help, this book would be far less informative and comprehensive than it is.

A thanks to Mike and Lida Giampola; Charles Ocheltree of the Spanish National Tourist Office in New York; Karen Weiner and Beth Verances of Weiner-Escalera Associates; Simon O'Hanlan of the Irish Tourist Board; Elizabether Robinson of Relais et Chateaux in Paris; Eric McFerran of BTH; Florentine Helbich and Beatrix of Dial Austria; Amerlia Ligouri Medweid and her staff at the Italian Government Travel Office; Andrew Glaze and Theresa Bunkerly of the British Tourist Authority; Enza Cirrincione of CIGA Hotels in New York; Ingrid Meyer of Romantik Hotels; Erica Faisst of the Swiss National Tourist Office; Hedy Wuerz and her staff at the German National Tourist Office; and the countless owners, proprietors, dukes, barons, princes, counts, and countesses who shared their love for historic places with us.

INTRODUCTION

Scattered across Europe are hundreds of castles, palaces, chateaux, manor houses, monasteries and historic buildings that have been converted into luxury hotels for the discriminate traveler in search of *something different*. For no more than you'd pay for an ordinary room in a sterile, glass-and-brick modern hotel, you can step inside and take that imaginary journey back in time when European royalty slept in palatial suites high above a castle's moat and dined at night to the strains of a 15th-century string quartet in a Victorian dining room.

Built hundreds of years ago as the residences of Europe's royalty or as fortresses against opponents of the church and throne, these hotels have maintained their old world atmosphere, yet still provide most of the modern conveniences. Rooms decorated in authentic antiques might have private bath, telephone, and television, but if getting away from modern conveniences is more appropriate, you can choose from hotels that offer what we classify as the *elegant basics*: a quiet room in a historic atmosphere with nary a modern convenience in sight. Many hotels offer rooms with or without bath (bathing facilities are down the hall), and almost all include a complimentary, continental breakfast in the room rate. Others offer optional demi-pension (two meals daily) or full-pension (all meals) plans, and substantial savings can be had by taking all of your meals at the hotel's restaurant.

You can choose from a stately, 17th-century Venetian palace hotel overlooking the Grand Canal in Venice; a 1700 hunting lodge hotel located high in the hills of Bavaria; a monastery hotel in Italy, surrounded by gardens filled with Roman headstones dating back to the third century or an elegant, fifty-room French chateau hotel, once the summer residence of the King of France. In Switzerland, you can sleep in a bedroom that once hosted Queen Victoria, dine where Napoleon dined, and stroll through spacious gardens once patrolled by Roman warriors. In Spain, you can reserve a Spanish Cardinal's suite with its massive, black marble tub, platformed canopy bed, and private chapel. Try an old Scottish castle hotel built in the 16th century as a retreat for Bonnie Prince Charles or a moated German castle hotel tucked in the foothills near the base of the Alps. In France, drive across an ancient wooden drawbridge into a cobblestoned courtyard alive with flowers where you're personally greeted by the owners, descendants of a 16th-century count and countess. At night, dine in a castle's restaurant located high in the castle's tower, surrounded by stone ramparts that still bear the scars of ancient battles.

Many of the owners of these historic hotels are direct descendants of the original builders, so it's not uncommon to be hosted in England by an authentic duke or in France by a titled baron, prince or countess who are proud of their family's history and what their hotels have to offer. In renovating these buildings, most have retained the original style and furnishings, so you'll find bedrooms decorated in Louis XIV, elegant sitting rooms displaying family coats of arms over massive stone fireplaces, and a wide range of room options—from single rooms converted from a former monk's cell to sprawling suites with terraced balconies overlooking the nearby village.

Lunch might be served in the inner courtyard behind stone walls, the former meeting place of Norman warriors and King's knights. Dinner is usually a more formal affair, served in a Victorian Hall, a ballroom decorated with crystal chandeliers and 14th-century, hand-painted murals or in a converted underground dungeon with walls cut out of solid rock and secret passages leading to the main building. The fare ranges from simple to elegant with an emphasis on regional dishes and (of course) continental cuisine, and many of these hotel restaurants are recipients of Europe's most prestigious culinary awards.

Exactly where these historic hotels are located and what they have to offer is the purpose of this guide. It contains information on locations, history, and facilities, along with names, addresses, and telephone numbers you can contact prior to leaving for Europe or after arrival. If you find yourself in the southeast corner of Switzerland and are ready for a special experience, just call ahead, make a reservation, and check in. En route to Italy, you might want to stop off at a chateau or castle hotel in France or detour south into Spain for some special experiences at Spain's paradors.

Often located well off the beaten tourist path, these hotels were built on strategic locations; high atop a mountain range overlooking the surrounding valley, in the quiet countryside miles from the nearest town or village or along the banks of a river or lake. Ideally, you'll have an automobile at your disposal and a good local map (Michelin makes the best) pinpointing Europe's smaller towns and cities. Many vacationers prefer using Europe's rail system, which is fast, efficient, and reaches out into every remote corner of Europe. Information on car rentals and bus and train travel is available from any of the European tourist offices listed in this guide.

Rates vary with the type of accommodations and the time of the year. Europe is basically a three-season vacationing area, with the low season (mid-October through February, except in ski resort areas) offering rates 20–30 percent lower than the high season. During the high season (June through August), reservations are highly recommended and can be obtained directly from the hotel or through any of the major U.S. and European representatives, some of which publish excellent hotel guides that are available free or at low cost.

The rates listed in this guide are listed in local currencies since they're more likely to remain fairly stable, while the U.S. dollar exchange rates fluctuate. All rates are current as of press time and are subject to change (and probably will), so we strongly suggest you request current rates prior to making your reservations.

The following currencies are used throughout this guide:

Austria
    1 Austrian schilling=5.69¢ $1=17.57 schillings

France
    1 French franc=14.54¢ $1=6.88 francs

West Germany
    1 German mark=40.1¢ $1=2.5 marks

England/Wales/Scotland
    1 English pound=$1.73 $1=.57 pounds

Scotland (also has its own currency)
    1 Scottish pound=$1.74 $1=.57 pounds

Ireland
    1 Irish pound=$1.38 $1=.72 pounds

Italy
    1 Italian lire=.075¢ $1=1338.69 lire

Spain
    1 Spanish peseta=.91¢ $1=109.9 pesetas

Switzerland
    1 Swiss franc=46.51¢ $1=2.15 francs

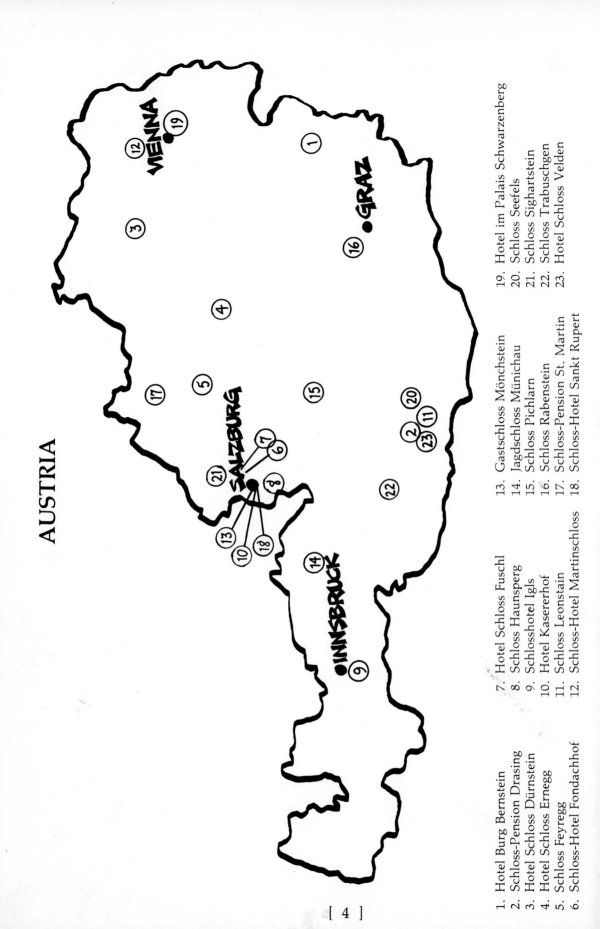

AUSTRIA

1. Hotel Burg Bernstein
2. Schloss-Pension Drasing
3. Hotel Schloss Dürnstein
4. Hotel Schloss Ernegg
5. Schloss Feyregg
6. Schloss-Hotel Fondachhof
7. Hotel Schloss Fuschl
8. Schloss Haunsperg
9. Schlosshotel Igls
10. Hotel Kasererhof
11. Schloss Leonstain
12. Schloss-Hotel Martinschloss
13. Gastschloss Mönchstein
14. Jagdschloss Münichau
15. Schloss Pichlarn
16. Schloss Rabenstein
17. Schloss-Pension St. Martin
18. Schloss-Hotel Sankt Rupert
19. Hotel im Palais Schwarzenberg
20. Schloss Seefels
21. Schloss Sighartstein
22. Schloss Trabuschgen
23. Hotel Schloss Velden

CONTENTS

Hotel Burg BERNSTEIN

Bernstein Castle stands at the top of a cliff overlooking the Tauchen Valley. The estate dates back to 860 A.D. when the area was owned by the Salzburg archbishop. During the twelfth century, the fortress was owned by Duke Friedrich II of Austria. Between 1336 and the early 1700s, the castle changed hands several times and in 1864 was purchased by Edward O'Egan, an Irishman. After the first World War, a factory for the production of jewelry and ornamental objects made from the translucent green stones found in this area was started by the Bernstein family. In 1952 Burg Bernstein opened as a hotel.

ADDRESS	Hotel Burg Bernstein
	Schlossweg 1
	A–7434 Bernstein
TELEPHONE	(05354) 220
NUMBER OF ROOMS	24 beds in 11 rooms, some with bath
OPEN	April to October 1
OWNER-MANAGER	Countess Maria Kuefstein
AGENCY	Dial Austria

Schloss-Pension DRASING

ADDRESS	Schloss-Pension Drasing A-9201 Krumpendorf/ Wörthersee
RATES	Single room with breakfast from 270AS per person per night during June and September, 300AS per night during July and August
OPEN	January to September
OWNER-MANAGER	Carlo and Irmingard Kos
AGENCY	Dial Austria

Hotel Schloss DÜRNSTEIN

Built in 1630, this early Baroque castle stands on a rocky terrace overlooking the Danube. Once the summer residence of the Princes of Starhemberg, it's been converted into a hotel with a gourmet restaurant, heated swimming pool, sauna, and solarium.

ADDRESS	Hotel Schloss Dürnstein A-3601 Dürnstein
TELEPHONE	(02711) 212
TELEX	071147

NUMBER OF ROOMS	75 beds in 33 rooms
RATES	Single room with bath and one meal daily from 520AS to 690AS per person. Double room with bath from 520AS to 645AS per person per day
OPEN	Mid-March to mid-November
OWNER-MANAGER	Johann Thiery
AGENCIES	Dial Austria, Relais et Châteaux

Hotel Schloss ERNEGG

This twelfth-century hotel lies in the foothills of the Austrian Alps and offers a commanding view of the Danube Valley. The estate was first mentioned in the year 979 when Emperor Otto gave the land between the Erlauf Rivers to Bishop Wolfgang of Regensburg. The building was converted into a fortress against the invading Turks and in 1675, the castle's chapel and buildings were restored. In the early 1700s, the castle came into the hands of the Auersperg family.

All of the twenty bedrooms have names relating to the castle's history, and the atmosphere here is more like a private home than a hotel. Special seven-day stays, including room, all meals, and daily green fees or one hour of horseback riding daily are available for 3450AS per person.

ADDRESS	Hotel Schloss Ernegg A–32–61 Steinakirchen am Forst
TELEPHONE	(07488) 214
TELEX	019298
NUMBER OF ROOMS	40 rooms, 18 with bath
RATES	Single room with bath and breakfast from 390AS per person per night between July and August, 290AS per person during May, June, September, and October
OPEN	May 1 through October
OWNER-MANAGER	Countess Hilda Maria Auersperg
AGENCY	Dial Austria

Schloss FEYREGG

Located about a mile outside the health resort of Bad Hall, Feyregg Castle was once the home of the abbots of an ancient monastery. The rooms are furnished in period antiques, and an excellent restaurant specializes in regional dishes. Transportation for hotel guests is available to and from Bad Hall for health-spa treatments.

ADDRESS	Schloss Feyregg A–4540 Bad Hall
TELEPHONE	(07258) 2591
NUMBER OF ROOMS	22 beds in 14 rooms
OPEN	January 7 through November 30
OWNER-MANAGER	Ruth Maria Harmer
AGENCY	Dial Austria

Schloss-Hotel FONDACHHOF

Built in the late 1700s, the Fondachhof is an Austrian manor house located at the foot of the Gaisberg. A hotel since 1950, it's located on parklands near the city of Salzburg and offers elegantly furnished rooms, heated swimming pools, and saunas.

ADDRESS	Schloss-Hotel Fondachhof Gaisbergstrasse 46 A–5020 Salzburg
TELEPHONE	(06222) 20906
NUMBER OF ROOMS	48 beds in 30 rooms
OPEN	April through October
OWNER-MANAGER	Dr. Kurt and Susanne Asamer
AGENCY	Dial Austria

Hotel Schloss FUSCHL

ADDRESS	Hotel Schloss Fuschl A–5322 Hof bei Salzburg
TELEPHONE	(06229) 253
TELEX	0633454
NUMBER OF ROOMS	58 rooms, 6 apartments
RATES	Single room with break-fast from 1,400AS to 1,800AS per person per night. Apartments from 2,400AS to 3,600AS per night
OPEN	Mid-April through October
OWNER-MANAGER	Max Grundig-Stiftung and U. Zellerbauer
AGENCIES	Dial Austria, Relaix et Châteaux

Schloss HAUNSPERG

Fifteen minutes by car from the center of Salzburg, Haunsperg Castle is a fourteenth-century historic building furnished with antiques dating back to the building's origin.

ADDRESS	Schloss Haunsperg Oberalm 32 A–5411 Oberalm/Hallein
TELEPHONE	(06245) 2662
NUMBER OF ROOMS	15 beds in 7 rooms, all with bath
OPEN	Year-round
OWNER-MANAGER	Dr. Emmerich von Gernerth
AGENCY	Dial Austria

Schlosshotel IGLS

The Igls was built between 1870 and 1880 and has been a hotel for fifteen years. It features beautifully appointed rooms, a hearthside bar, a restaurant with gold-velveteen furnishings, and a glass-enclosed swimming pool. Stretching out around the hotel are acres of lawn surrounded by towering trees.

ADDRESS	Schlosshotel Igls
	A–6080 Igls
TELEPHONE	(05222) 77217
TELEX	053314
NUMBER OF ROOMS	30 beds in 16 rooms with bath
RATES	Double room with bath from 540AS to 830AS. Suites from 820AS to 1100AS. Room with bath and full board from 610AS per person per night
OPEN	December to November
OWNER-MANAGER	Dr. Stephan Beck
AGENCY	Dial Austria

Hotel KASERERHOF

The first record of Kasererhof Castle dates back to the fourteenth century when the estate belonged to an Austrian archbishop. In 1642 the mansion was built, and in 1677 the current chapel was erected to the left of the main entrance hall. During the mid-1800s, the castle was named Kasererhof and became the center of festival activities in the surrounding area. Since 1929, the Gunther Strohbichler family has been managing the estate. In the chapel, a carved crucifixion group dating back to 1742 is on display, and an altar piece, dated 1712, shows the old town of Salzburg and the Kasererhof as they were during the fourteenth century.

ADDRESS	Hotel Kasererhof
	Alpenstrasse 6
	A–5020 Salzburg
TELEPHONE	(06222) 21265
TELEX	063477
OPEN	Year-round
OWNER-MANAGER	Gunther-Strohbichler Family

Schloss LEONSTAIN

ADDRESS	Schloss Leonstain Hauptstrasse 28 A–9210 Pörtschach/ Wörthersee
TELEPHONE	(04272) 2816
TELEX	042019
NUMBER OF ROOMS	71 beds in 30 rooms, all with bath
OPEN	May 10 to September 30
OWNER-MANAGER	Aldo Neuscheller
AGENCY	Dial Austria

Schloss-Hotel MARTINSCHLOSS

Built in the mid-1700s, Martin Castle is a beautiful example of Austrian Baroque architecture. Between 1920 and 1924, the castle served as the home of the Trapp family of *Sound of Music* fame, and portions of the film were shot here.

ADDRESS	Schloss-Hotel Martinschloss Martinstrasse 34–36 A–3400 Klosterneuburg
TELEPHONE	(02243) 7426
TELEX	074257
NUMBER OF ROOMS	75 beds in 60 rooms, all with bath

OPEN	Year-round
OWNER-MANAGER	Dr. Emmer-Reissig
AGENCIES	Dial Austria, Relais du Silence

Gastschloss MÖNCHSTEIN

Mönchstein Castle was built in 1358 on the Mönchsberg, a mountain that lies in the heart of the city of Salzburg. Originally built for the guests of the archbishop, in 1622 it became the estate of the Monastery of Mulin. The chapel of the castle is mentioned in documents dating back to the early 1500s. Baron Leitner, a banker in Salzburg, was one of the original owners of Mönchstein, and he installed an elevator that scaled the sheer rocks surrounding the castle. In 1918 the castle was sold and completely remodeled, and it opened as a hotel in 1948.

ADDRESS	Gastschloss Mönchstein Mönchsberg 26 A-5020 Salzburg
TELEPHONE	(06222) 41363
TELEX	632080
NUMBER OF ROOMS	25 beds in 12 rooms, all with bath
RATES	Single room with bath from 500AS to 600AS per person per night. Double rooms with bath from 450AS to 750AS per person per night
OPEN	Year-round
OWNER-MANAGER	Karl Mierka
AGENCY	Dial Austria

Jagdschloss MÜNICHAU

ADDRESS	Jagdschloss Münichau A-6370 Kitzbühel
TELEPHONE	(05356) 2962
TELEX	51396
NUMBER OF ROOMS	80 beds in 35 rooms
OPEN	May 20 to October 1 and December 15 to Easter

OWNER-MANAGER	The Harisch Family
AGENCY	Dial Austria

Schloss PICHLARN

ADDRESS	Schloss Pichlarn
	A–8952 Irdning
TELEPHONE	(03682) 2841
TELEX	038190
NUMBER OF ROOMS	130 beds in 76 rooms, all with bath
OPEN	Year-round
AGENCY	Dial Austria

Schloss RABENSTEIN

Set on a cliff overlooking the Mur Valley, Rabenstein Castle is one of the oldest fortresses in Styria. It houses a large collection of art works, and all rooms are furnished with period antiques. The courtyard with fountains and two sun terraces overlooks the valley, and chamber music concerts are held in the castle's Grand Hall during June.

ADDRESS	Schloss Rabenstein
	Adriach 41
	A–8130 Frohnleiten
TELEPHONE	(03126) 2303
NUMBER OF ROOMS	8 beds in 5 rooms, all with bath
OWNER-MANAGER	Sigurt Reininghaus
AGENCY	Dial Austria

Schloss-Pension ST. MARTIN

Built in the eleventh century, St. Martin Castle is set in unspoiled forests in the Innviertel region, near the border between Austria and Bavaria.

ADDRESS	Schloss-Pension St. Martin
	A–4973 St. Martin im Innkreis
TELEPHONE	(07751) 6102

NUMBER OF ROOMS	42 beds in 23 rooms, all with bath
OPEN	Year-round
OWNER-MANAGER	Count Arco-Zinneberg
AGENCY	Dial Austria

Schloss-Hotel SANKT RUPERT

Once the property of a knightly order and the seat of several Austrian noble families, the St. Rupert was transformed into a hotel in 1952. Located five minutes from Salzburg, the hotel sits in spacious parklands surrounded by trees.

ADDRESS	Schloss-Hotel Sankt Rupert
	Morzgerstrasse 31
	A–5020 Salzburg
TELEPHONE	(06222) 43231
NUMBER OF ROOMS	55 beds in 26 rooms, all with bath
OPEN	April 1 to October 1
OWNER-MANAGER	Marto Steinbacher
AGENCY	Dial Austria

Hotel im Palais SCHWARZENBERG

ADDRESS	Hotel im Palais Schwarzenberg
	Schwarzenbergplatz 9
	A–1030 Vienna
TELEPHONE	(0222) 784515
TELEX	136124
NUMBER OF ROOMS	80 beds in 44 rooms with bath
OPEN	Year-round
OWNER-MANAGER	Prince Karl Johannes von Schwarzenberg
AGENCIES	Dial Austria, Relais et Châteaux

Schloss SEEFELS

The Seefels (Lake Rock) Castle Hotel has its own quarter-mile private beach on the Wörthersee. Situated in a thirty-seven-acre park, the hotel has a golf course nearby, facilities for boating, and its own private therapy center.

ADDRESS	Schloss Seefels
	A–9210 Pörtschach/Wörthersee
TELEPHONE	(04272) 2377
TELEX	042153
NUMBER OF ROOMS	70 rooms with bath
OPEN	April 30 to mid-October
OWNER-MANAGER	N. Dumba
AGENCIES	Dial Austria, Relais et Châteaux

Schloss SIGHARTSTEIN

For over six hundred years, Sighartstein Castle has been in the possession of the Counts of Uiberacker. Since 1962, the castle has been owned by the daughter of the last count, the Countess Gabrielle Palffy. Suits of armor, period furniture, and paintings decorate the castle's Grand Hall, and all rooms are furnished in the original style. Set in parklands and forests, the castle is located fourteen miles off the Salzburg-Vienna main highway.

ADDRESS	Schloss Sighartstein
	A5202 Neumarkt bei Salzburg
TELEPHONE	(06216) 251
NUMBER OF ROOMS	13 beds in 9 rooms, all with bath
OPEN	April 15 to October 15
OWNER-MANAGER	Count and Countess Joseph Palffy
AGENCY	Dial Austria

Schloss TRABUSCHGEN

ADDRESS	Schloss Trabuschgen A–9821 Obervellach bei Mallnitz
TELEPHONE	(04782) 2042
RATES	Room with bath and two meals daily from 210AS to 270AS per person per day
OPEN	Year-round

Hotel Schloss VELDEN

The Velden Castle Hotel sits in a large park on the shores of a lake with private beach and has its own gambling casino.

ADDRESS	Hotel Schloss Velden Am Korso 24 A–9220 Velden
TELEPHONE	(04274) 2655
NUMBER OF ROOMS	180 beds in 110 rooms
OPEN	May 1 to October 1
OWNER-MANAGER	Sophie Bunzel and Elsa Bohm
AGENCY	Dial Austria

FRANCE

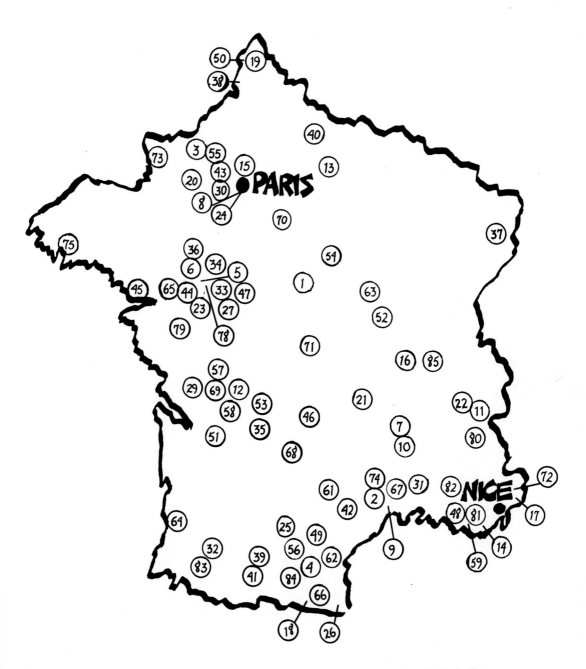

1. L'Abbaye de Saint-Michel
2. Château d'Adoult
3. Château d'Audrieu
4. Domaine d'Auriac
5. Château de Beaulieu
6. Domaine de Beauvois
7. Château du Besset
8. La Résidence de Bois
9. Le Cabro d'Or
10. Le Capitelle

11. Château de Challes
12. La Chappele de
    Saint-Martin
13. Hostellerie du Château
14. Domaine de Chateauneuf
15. Château de Chaumontel
16. Château de Chervinges
17. Château de la
    Chevre d'Or
18. Hôtel de la Cité

19. Grand Hôtel Clement
20. Hostellerie du Clos
21. Château de Codignat
22. Château de Collonges
23. Domaine de la Cortinière
24. Hôtel Crillon
25. L'Ecluse
26. Castel Emeraude
27. Hotel d'Espagne
28. L'Esperance

CONTENTS

L'ABBAYE DE SAINT-MICHEL

A former Benedictine abbey dating back to the thirteenth century.

Address	L'Abbaye de Saint-Michael 89700 Tonnerre (Yonne)
Telephone	(86) 55 05 99
Number of Rooms	7 rooms, 3 apartments
Rates	Single room with bath from 270F to 440F. Apartments from 600F to 750 F
Open	January 31 to December 20
Owner-Manager	Daniel Cussac
Agency	Relais et Châteaux

Château d'AGOULT

Address	Hôtel Marie d'Agoult (Château d'Arpaillargues) 30700 Uzes (Gard)
Telephone	(66) 22 14 48
Number of Rooms	24 rooms and 2 apartments
Rates	Single room for 120F to 210F
Open	March 1 to January 4
Owner-Manager	G. Savry
Agency	Relais du Silence

Château d'AUDRIEU

Address	Château d'Audrieu Tilly-sur-Seulles 14250 Audrieu (Calvados)
Telephone	(31) 80 21 52
Telex	170234
Number of Rooms	18 rooms, 4 apartments
Rates	Single rooms from 280F to 440F per person per night. Suites from 440F to 696F per night
Open	March 16 through November
Owner-Manager	Mrs. Livry-Level

Domaine d'AURIAC

ADDRESS	Domaine d'Auriac
	Route de St. Hilaire
	11000 Carcassonne (Aude)
TELEPHONE	(68) 25 72 22
TELEX	500385
NUMBER OF ROOMS	23 rooms
RATES	Single room with bath from 180F to 300F per person per night
OPEN	Year-round except January 15 to 30
OWNER-MANAGER	Mr. and Mrs. Rigaudis
AGENCY	Relais et Châteaux

Château de BEAULIEU

ADDRESS	Château de Beaulieu
	Joue les Tours
	37300 Tours (Indre-et-Loire)
TELEPHONE	(47) 28 52 19
NUMBER OF ROOMS	17 rooms
RATES	Single room from 55F to 170F
OPEN	Year-round
OWNER-MANAGER	J. P. Lozay

Domaine de BEAUVOIS

ADDRESS	Domaine de Beauvois
	Route de Clere
	37230 Luynes (Indre-et-Loire)
TELEPHONE	(47) 55 50 11
TELEX	750204
NUMBER OF ROOMS	35 rooms, 5 apartments, 2 villas
RATES	Single room from 220F to 520F. Apartments from 595F to 850F
OPEN	Mid-March to mid-January
OWNER-MANAGER	P. Ponsard and Rene Traversac

Château du BESSET

ADDRESS	Château du Besset 07130 St. Romain de Lerps (Ardèche)
TELEPHONE	(75) 44 41 63
NUMBER OF ROOMS	6 rooms, 4 apartments
RATES	Single room with bath and breakfast from 800F to 900F. Apartments from 1100F to 1300F
OPEN	March 29 to October 10
OWNER-MANAGER	Mr. and Mrs. Gozlan and Mrs. De Leon
AGENCY	Relais et Châteaux

La Résidence de BOIS

ADDRESS	La Residence de Bois 16 Rue Chalgrin 75116 Paris
TELEPHONE	500 50 59
Number of Rooms	17 rooms, 3 apartments
RATES	Single room with bath from 460F to 710F. Apartments from 750F to 850F
OPEN	Year-round
OWNER-MANAGER	Mr. and Mrs. Desponts
AGENCY	Relais et Château

Le CABRO D'OR

ADDRESS	Le Cabro d'Or 13520 Les Baux-de-Provence (Bouches-du-Rhône)
TELEPHONE	(90) 97 33 21
TELEX	401810
NUMBER OF ROOMS	19 rooms

RATES	Single rooms from 250F to 390F
OPEN	Year-round except November 15 and December 20
OWNER-MANAGER	Mr. Thuiler and Mrs. Moscoloni
AGENCY	Relais et Châteaux

Le CAPITELLE

ADDRESS	Le Capitelle Marmande 26270 Loriol (Drome)
TELEPHONE	(75) 61 02 72
NUMBER OF ROOMS	15 beds in rooms and suites
RATES	Single room from 62F to 120F. Suites from 150F to 210F
OPEN	March 17 to October 1
OWNER-MANAGER	Dancenis et Ferret
AGENCY	Relais du Silence

Château de CHALLES

ADDRESS	Château de Challes 73190 Challes-les-Eaux (Savoie)
TELEPHONE	(79) 25 11 45
NUMBER OF ROOMS	70 rooms
OPEN	Year-round
OWNER-MANAGER	Maurice Biette

La CHAPELLE DE SAINT-MARTIN

ADDRESS	La Chapelle de Saint-Martin Nieul-près-Limoges 87510 Saint-Martin (Haute-Vienne)
TELEPHONE	(55) 75 80 17
NUMBER OF ROOMS	9 rooms

RATES	Single room from 190F to 250F per person per night
OPEN	Year-round
OWNER-MANAGER	M. Jacques Dudognon

Hostellerie du CHATEAU

ADDRESS	Hostellerie du Château Beaumes de Venise 84190 Carpentras (Vaucluse)
TELEPHONE	(90) 65 00 21
NUMBER OF ROOMS	20 rooms
RATES	Single room from 65F to 143F
OPEN	January 1 to October 31
OWNER-MANAGER	S. A. LeMajoral
AGENCY	Relais du Silence

Domaine de CHATEAUNEUF

ADDRESS	Domaine de Chateauneuf Le Sainte Baume 83860 Nans-les-Pins (Provence)
TELEPHONE	(94) 78 90 06
TELEX	400747
NUMBER OF ROOMS	16 rooms, 3 apartments
RATES	Single room with bath from 240F to 335F per person per night. Apartments from 475F to 505F per night
OPEN	April 1 to December 12
OWNER-MANAGER	M. Jacques Malet
AGENCY	Relais et Châteaux

Château de CHAUMONTEL

The Château de Chaumontel is a sixteenth-century castle hotel surrounded by water, forests, and gardens and located about fifteen miles from Paris.

ADDRESS	Château de Chaumontel
	95270 Luzarches (Val-d'Oise)
TELEPHONE	(16 3) 471 03 51
NUMBER OF ROOMS	40 rooms, 1 apartment
RATES	Single room with bath from 135F to 175F. Apartment from 320F
OPEN	Year-round
OWNER-MANAGER	Michel and Irene Bondon

Château de CHERVINGES

ADDRESS	Château de Chervinges
	69400 Villefranche sur Saône (Rhône)
TELEPHONE	(74) 65 29 76
NUMBER OF ROOMS	11 beds
RATES	Single room from 180F to 300F
AGENCY	Relais du Silence

Château de la CHEVRE d'OR

ADDRESS	Château de la Chevre d'Or Côte d'Azur 06360 Eze-Village (Alpes-Maritimes)
TELEPHONE	(93) 41 12 12
TELEX	460000–96
NUMBER OF ROOMS	6 rooms, 3 apartments
RATES	Single room from 450F to 600F. Apartments from 600F to 750F
OPEN	Mid-February to mid-November
OWNER-MANAGER	S. A. Bruno Ingold
AGENCY	Relais et Châteaux

Hôtel del la CITE

The hotel opened in September of 1909 and was enlarged in 1913 and 1927. It stands on the site of the former Bishop's Palace where popes, bishops, kings, and queens lived between the tenth and thirteenth centuries. Part of an elaborate fortress that overwhelms the town of Carcassonne, the hotel is surrounded by a moat with drawbridge that opens onto spacious courts with towers and ramparts. The Cathedral of St. Nazaire lies in the southwestern corner of the complex. The rooms are furnished in period antiques with four-poster beds.

ADDRESS	Hôtel de la Cité
	Place de l'Eglise
	11000 Carcassonne (Aude)
TELEPHONE	(16) 68 25 03 34
RATES	Single room with breakfast and bath from 125F to 391F per person per night. Double room with bath and breakfast from 231F to 419F per night
OPEN	Year-round
OWNER-MANAGER	Madame Dominique Lasserre

Grand Hôtel CLEMENT

ADDRESS	Grand Hôtel Clément
	62610 Ardres (Pas-de-Calais)
TELEPHONE	(21) 35 40 66
NUMBER OF ROOMS	19 beds
RATES	Single room from 40F to 100F
OPEN	February 15 to January 1
OWNER-MANAGER	P. Coolen
AGENCY	Relais du Silence

Hostellerie du CLOS

ADDRESS	Hostellerie du Clos
	98 Rue de la Ferté-Vidame
	27130 Verneuil-sur-Avre (Eure)
TELEPHONE	(32) 32 21 81
NUMBER OF ROOMS	9 rooms, 2 apartments
RATES	Single room from 210F to 290F. Apartments from 350F
OPEN	January 20 to December 15

OWNER-MANAGER	Patrick and Colette Simon
AGENCY	Relais et Châteaux

Château de CODIGNAT

ADDRESS	Château de Codignat Bort l'Etang 63190 Lezoux (Puy-de-Dome)
TELEPHONE	(73) 70 43 03
TELEX	990606
NUMBER OF ROOMS	11 rooms, 3 apartments
RATES	Single room with bath and breakfast from 300F to 450F per person per night. Apartments from 390F to 530F per night
OPEN	March 1 to November 3
OWNER-MANAGER	Barberan-M. G. Vidal and Monique Barberan

Château de COLLONGES

ADDRESS	Château de Collonges 73310 Ruffieux (Savoie)
TELEPHONE	(79) 63 27 38
NUMBER OF ROOMS	12 rooms
RATES	Single room with breakfast from 96F to 179F per person per night
OPEN	March 15 to November 15
OWNER-MANAGER	The Breysse and Carriere Families
AGENCY	Relais du Silence

Domaine de la CORTINIERE

ADDRESS	Domaine de la Cortinière 37250 Montblazon-et-Touraine

TELEPHONE	(47) 26 00 19
TELEX	750806
NUMBER OF ROOMS	21 rooms, 11 in the chateau, 10 in three pavilions
RATES	Twin bedded room with bath from 440F. Double rooms with bath from 375F per person per night. Suites from 565F per night
OPEN	Year-round
OWNER-MANAGER	D. Olivereau-Capron

Hôtel CRILLON

An elegant eighteenth-century hotel located in downtown Paris.

ADDRESS	Hôtel Crillon 10 Place de la Concorde 75008 Paris
TELEPHONE	296 10 81
TELEX	290204
NUMBER OF ROOMS	208 rooms, 39 apartments
RATES	Single room with bath and breakfast from 935F to 985F. Apartments from 1300F to 1650F
OPEN	Year-round
OWNER-MANAGER	Philippe Roche
AGENCY	Relais et Châteaux

L'ECLUSE

ADDRESS	L'Ecluse Perigueux 24420 Antonne (Dordogne)
TELEPHONE	(53) 06 00 04
NUMBER OF ROOMS	50 beds
RATES	Single room from 65F to 120F
OPEN	Year-round
OWNER-MANAGER	M. Beaugier

Castel EMERAUDE

ADDRESS	Castel Emeraude
	66110 Amelie-les-Bains
	(Pyrénées-Orientales)
TELEPHONE	(69) 39 02 83
NUMBER OF ROOMS	28 rooms
RATES	Single room with breakfast
	from 60F
OPEN	Year-round
OWNER-MANAGER	L. More
AGENCY	Relais du Silence

Hotel d'ESPAGNE

ADDRESS	Hotel d'Espagne
	8 Reu du Château
	3660 Valençay (Indre)
TELEPHONE	(54) 00 00 02
TELEX	751675
NUMBER OF ROOMS	10 rooms, 8 apartments
RATES	Single room from 180F to 300F
	per person per night. Apart-
	ments from 450F to 500F
OPEN	February 15 to December 14
OWNER-MANAGER	M. Fourre

L'ESPERANCE

ADDRESS	L'Esperance
	89450 Saint-Père-sous-Vezelay
TELEPHONE	(86) 32 20 45
NUMBER OF ROOMS	18 rooms, 1 apartment
RATES	Single room with breakfast
	from 200F
OPEN	February through December
OWNER-MANAGER	Mr. and Mrs. Meneau

Hostellerie du Domaine de FLEURAC

ADDRESS	Hostellerie du Domaine de Fleurac
	Fleurac, 16200 Jarnac (Charente)
TELEPHONE	(45) 81 78 22
NUMBER OF ROOMS	18 beds
RATES	Single room from 96F to 120F
OPEN	October 31 to November 15
OWNER-MANAGER	M. Guichemerre

Hôtel la FORESTIERE

ADDRESS	Hôtel la Forestiere
	1 Avenue Kennedy
	78100 Saint-Germain-en-Laye (Seine-et-Oise)
TELEPHONE	(3) 973 36 60
TELEX	696055
NUMBER OF ROOMS	24 rooms, 6 apartments
RATES	Single room from 280F to 350F. Apartments from 360F to 420F
OPEN	Year-round
OWNER-MANAGER	Mr. and Mrs. P. Cazaudehore

Hôtel les FRENES

ADDRESS	Hôtel les Frênes
	Avenue Vertes-Rives
	84140 Avignon-Montfavet (Vaucluse)
TELEPHONE	(90) 31 17 93
TELEX	431164
NUMBER OF ROOMS	18 rooms
RATES	Room with bath from 225F to 565F per person per night
OPEN	March through November
OWNER-MANAGER	M. Biancone
AGENCY	Relais et Châteaux

Bastide GASCONNE

ADDRESS	Bastide Gasconne
	Barbotan-les-Thermes
	32150 Cazaubon (Gers)
TELEPHONE	(62) 09 52 09
TELEX	521009
NUMBER OF ROOMS	49 rooms, 2 apartments
RATES	Single room with bath from 270F to 330F. Apartments from 380F to 620 F per night
OPEN	March 1 to November 1
AGENCY	Relais et Châteaux

Chateau du GUE-PEAN

The chateau's site on the edge of the Forest of Choussy was originally occupied by a hunting lodge that later became a stronghold fortress against the Normans. One of the most beautiful chateaux in France, it features a great tower overlooking fortified walls and a rectangular court yard bordered by two Renaissance pavilions dating back to the days of Henry II. Rooms are furnished with Louis XV and XVI furniture, tapestries, and paintings of former owners, and a library-museum displays a valuable collection of autographs and historic sourvenirs. In the Great Hall, a fireplace designed by Germain Pilon dominates the room. The present owners, descendants of the Counts of Apremont, have turned this chateau into an elegant hotel.

ADDRESS	Chateau du Gué-Péan
	Monthou-sur-Cher
	41400 Montrichard (Loir-et-Cher)
TELEPHONE	(16) 54 71 43 01
RATES	Single room with bath or shower from 126F to 195F. Single room with bath and two meals from 265F to 415F. Single room with all meals from 380F to 598F per person per day
OPEN	Year-round
OWNER-MANAGER	The Marquis de Keguelin

Domaine des HAUTS-DE-LOIRE

ADDRESS	Domaine des Hauts-de-Loire
	41150 Onzain (Loir-et-Cher)
TELEPHONE	(54) 79 72 57
NUMBER OF ROOMS	22 rooms, 8 apartments
RATES	Single rooms from 350F to
	550F. Apartments from 660F to
	750F
OPEN	March 2 to December 14
OWNER-MANAGER	P. A. Bonnigal

La HOIRIE

ADDRESS	La Hoirie
	24200 Sariat (Dordogne)
TELEPHONE	(53) 59 05 62
NUMBER OF ROOMS	15 beds
RATES	Single rooms from 95F to 150F
	per person per night
OPEN	March 15 to November 1
OWNER-MANAGER	M. Civel
AGENCY	Relais du Silence

Château d'IGE

ADDRESS	Château d'Igé
	71960 Ige (Saône-et-Loire)
TELEPHONE	(85) 33 33 99
NUMBER OF ROOMS	6 rooms, 5 apartments
RATES	Single rooms from 170F to
	280F. Apartments from 320F to
	390F
OPEN	December 16 to November 5
OWNER-MANAGER	Mr. and Mrs. Rodrigues

Château d'ISENBOURG

The chateau stands atop Gallibuhl hill, overlooking the town of Rouffach, the Black Forest and the Swiss Alps. The Isenbourg area was occupied in early times as an advance post for the military and the chateau itself was once the royal residence. Dagobert II, King of Austriasia, left the chateau and the surrounding estate in a charter written in 662AD.

In 1278 Bishop Conrad of Lichtenberg restored the walls and ditches around Isenbourg, and in 1380 the chateau was connected to the walls to establish an elaborate defense system. In 1791 Isenbourg was sold as public property, and in 1822 the old building was torn down and replaced by a country house. Between 1894 and 1895, towers were added at the southern end of the building, and an entire wing was built at the north end of the chateau. The remains of the old vaulted ceilings, dating from the fifteenth and sixteenth centuries, now decorate the restaurant and kitchen. In the Caveau des Princes Eveques room, traces of engravings are still visible, dating back to the year 1298.

Surrounded by its own vineyards, the Château d'Isenbourg has an outdoor heated swimming pool and tennis courts.

ADDRESS	Château d'Isenbourg
	68250 Rouffach (Haut-Rhin)
TELEPHONE	(89) 49 63 53
TELEX	880666
NUMBER OF ROOMS	19 double rooms with bath, 1 apartment
RATES	Single room with bath from 225F to 390F per person per night. Apartment from 520F to 540F per night
OPEN	Year-round except January 10 to March 13
OWNER-MANAGER	Daniel Dalibert

Pavillon JOINVILLE

ADDRESS	Pavillon Joinville
	76260 Eu-Le Tréport (Seine-Maritime)
TELEPHONE	(35) 86 24 03
NUMBER OF ROOMS	11 beds

RATES	Single room from 140F per person per night
OPEN	Year-round
OWNER-MANAGER	G. Eloy

Château de LARROQUE

ADDRESS	Château de Larroque Route de Toulouse 32200 Gimont (Gers)
TELEPHONE	(62) 67 77 44
NUMBER OF ROOMS	10 rooms, 2 apartments
RATES	Single room from 180F to 300F per person per night
OPEN	February 1 to January 1
OWNER-MANAGER	Celestin Fagedet
AGENCY	Relais et Châteaux

Château de LIGNY

A thirteenth-century chateau, surrounded by walls and towers.

ADDRESS	Château de Ligny Entrée du Park 59191 Ligny-Haucourt (Nord)
TELEPHONE	(27) 85 25 84
TELEX	820211
NUMBER OF ROOMS	7 rooms, 3 apartments
RATES	Single room from 280F to 350F. Apartments from 400F to 700F
OPEN	February 1 to January 1
OWNER-MANAGER	M. Andre Blot and Mr. and Mrs. Galan

Château de LOCQUENOLE

ADDRESS	Château de Locquenolé Route de Port-Louis 56700 Hennebont (Morbihan)

TELEPHONE	(97) 76 29 04
TELEX	740853
NUMBER OF ROOMS	38 rooms, 3 apartments
RATES	Single room from 200F to 443 F. Apartments from 450F to 664F
OPEN	March 11 to November 30
OWNER-MANAGER	Mrs. de la Sabliere
AGENCY	Relais et Châteaux

Château de la MALENE

Once the residence of the De Montequiou family, the Castle de la Malène is located in the Gorges of Tarn. With terraces and gardens and a restaurant specializing in regional dishes, the chateau is furnished in period antiques with four-poster beds in most rooms.

ADDRESS	Château de la Malène 48210 La Malène (Lozere)
TELEPHONE	(66) 48 51 12
NUMBER OF ROOMS	10 rooms and apartments
OPEN	May 1 to October 15

Le MANOIR

An elegant chateau-hotel located about thirty minutes by car from Paris.

ADDRESS	Le Manoir
	Route Départementale 402
	77610 Fontenay-Trésigny
TELEPHONE	(6) 409 21 17
NUMBER OF ROOMS	11 rooms, 2 apartments
RATES	Single room with bath from
	250F to 380F. Apartments from
	460 F
OPEN	March 17 to Janaury 1
OWNER-MANAGER	M. P. Sourisseau
AGENCY	Relais et Châteaux

Château de MARÇAY

Set in the middle of farmlands and vineyards, the Château de Marçay was built in 1150 as a military fortress. Connected to nearby chateaux by underground passages, it was mostly destroyed during the 1534 Religious War by the Huguenots. Partially rebuilt, then destroyed again by soldiers of Geoffroy de la Tremoille, it was again rebuilt and managed to survive the French Revolution in 1789. Two underground passages, one starting in the chateau's wine cellar deep underground and another from the outside wall are still accessible.

Monsieur Luc Gilbert de Fontenay bought the chateau and surrounding land hundreds of years ago. In 1968, the Château de Marçay opened as a hotel.

ADDRESS	Château de Marçay
	37500 Chinon (Indre-et-Loire)
TELEPHONE	(47) 93 03 47
TELEX	750806
NUMBER OF ROOMS	26 rooms with bath, 15 in the main building, 11 in the annex
RATES	Single room with bath from 280F to 580F per person per night in the main building, from 215F to 350F per night in the annex
OPEN	March 5 to January 5
OWNER-MANAGER	Philippe Mollard and J. Luc Hatet
AGENCY	Relais et Châteaux

Castel MARIE-LOUISE

ADDRESS	Castel Marie-Louise Esplanade du Casino 44504 La Baule (Morbihan)
TELEPHONE	(40) 60 20 60
TELEX	710510
NUMBER OF ROOMS	29 rooms, 2 apartments
RATES	Single room from 300F. Apartments from 500F to 900F per night
OPEN	February 10 to January 5
OWNER-MANAGER	Lucien Barriere
AGENCY	Relais et Châteaux

La MARONNE

ADDRESS	La Maronne 15140 Saint-Martin-Valmeroux Salers (Cantal)
TELEPHONE	(71) 69 20 33
NUMBER OF ROOMS	44 beds
RATES	Single room from 50F to 90F
OPEN	December 15 to August 30
OWNER-MANAGER	J. Souchal and D. Guesne
AGENCY	Relais du Silence

Les MEAULNES

ADDRESS	Les Meaulnes 18330 Nançay (Cher)
TELEPHONE	(48) 51 81 15
NUMBER OF ROOMS	10 rooms
RATES	Single room with bath from 175F to 210F
OPEN	Mid-February to mid-January
OWNER-MANAGER	Mr. and Mrs. Mascheroni

Château de MEYRARGUES

The Château de Meyrargues is considered to be one of France's oldest fortified sites, dating back to 600 B.C. when it was a Celtic outpost. The entranceway reflects off a pool with twin, high stone towers flanking a sweeping, balustraded set of stairs. From its terraces and rooms you can get a panoramic view of the Valley of the Durance. Now the home of the Drouillet Family, the Lords of Les Baux once lived here. All of the rooms vary in size, view, and decor, but most are furnished in period antiques. During the high season, all rooms are only available with the demi-pension (two meals) option.

In 1291, Hugues des Boux sold the chateau to the Count of Provence, and it changed hands many times over the coming years. In 1430, Queen Yolande, the widow of Louis II, owned the chateau, and upon her death King Rene passed it on to Artaluche D'Alagonia for services rendered during the Wars of Italy. In 1649, the chateau was partially destroyed by shelling and fire. It's been a hotel since 1952.

ADDRESS	Château de Meyrargues
	Route de Chateau
	13650 Meyrargues
	(Bouches-du-Rhône)
TELEPHONE	(42) 57 50 32
NUMBER OF ROOMS	14 rooms
RATES	Single room with bath from 175F to 275F. Double room with bath from 160F to 250F per night
OPEN	Year-round except December through February
OWNER-MANAGER	Jeanne Drouillet

Château de MONTLEDIER

ADDRESS	Château de Montlédier
	Route d'Angles
	81660 Mazamet (Tarn)
TELEPHONE	(63) 61 20 54
NUMBER OF ROOMS	10 rooms
RATES	Single room from 220F to 320F per person per night

Hotel Schloss Ernegg, *Austria*

Hotel Schloss Fuschl, *Austria*

Schloss-Pension Drasing, *Austria*

Schloss Seefels, *Austria*

Gastschloss Mönchstein, *Austria*

chloss Haunsperg, *Austria*

Le Domaine de la Tortinière, *France*

chloss Trabuschgen, *Austria*

Château de la Malène, *France*

Château de Chaumontel, *France*

Château d'Isenbourg, *France*

Château de Chaumontel, *France*

Château de Malène, *France*

Château de Roumégouse, *France*

Château de Malène, *France*

Château de Marçay, *France*

Château du Gué-Péan, *France*
Château de Rochegude, *France*

OPEN	Year-round except January and March
OWNER-MANAGER	Mr. and Mrs. F. Sidobre

Château de MONTREUIL

ADDRESS	Château de Montreuil 4 Chaussée-des-Capucins 62170 Montreuil-sur-Mer (Pas-de-Calais)
TELEPHONE	(21) 06 00 11
NUMBER OF ROOMS	12 rooms
RATES	Single room from 220F to 330F
OPEN	Year-round except Christmas, January 3, and January 31

Hostellerie du MOULIN DE L'ABBAYE

ADDRESS	Hostellerie du Moulin de l'Abbaye Route de Bourgeilles 24310 Brantôme-en-Périgord (Dordogne)
TELEPHONE	(53) 05 80 22
TELEX	560570
NUMBER OF ROOMS	8 rooms, 2 apartments
RATES	Single room with bath from 240F to 310F. Apartments from 350F
OPEN	Mid-May to mid-October
OWNER-MANAGER	Kate and Regis Bulot
AGENCY	Relais et Châteaux

MOULIN D'HAUTERIVE

ADDRESS	Moulin d'Hauterive St.-Gervais-en-Vallière 71350 Beaune (Côte-d'Or)

TELEPHONE	(85) 42 55 66
NUMBER OF ROOMS	36 beds
RATES	Single room from 70F to 120F per person per night
OPEN	March 15 to January 1
OWNER-MANAGER	Moille et Dauvergne

MOULIN DU ROC

ADDRESS	Moulin du Roc 24530 Champagnac-de-Belair (Dordogne)
TELEPHONE	(53) 54 80 36
TELEX	570335
NUMBER OF ROOMS	7 rooms, 1 apartment
RATES	Single room from 210F to 260F. Apartments from 300F
OPEN	Year-round
OWNER-MANAGER	Mr. and Mrs. Gardilou

Hostellerie du MOULIN DES RUATS

ADDRESS	Hostellerie du Moulin des Ruats Vallée du Cousin 8920 Avallon (Yonne)
TELEPHONE	(86) 34 07 14
NUMBER OF ROOMS	21 rooms, most with bath
RATES	Single room from 120F to 200F
OPEN	January 3 to October 30
OWNER-MANAGER	Mr. and Mrs. Bertier

Hostellerie du MOULIN DE VILLERAY

ADDRESS	Hostellerie du Moulin de Villeray 61110 Condau (Ome)
TELEPHONE	(33) 33 30 32
NUMBER OF ROOMS	10 rooms
RATES	Single room from 290F to 360F

| OPEN | February 1 to December 12 |
| OWNER-MANAGER | Mr. and Mrs. Coldeboeuf |

La MUSARDIERE

ADDRESS	La Musardière
	34 Avenue de la République
	12100 Millau (Aveyron)
TELEPHONE	(65) 60 20 63
NUMBER OF ROOMS	12 rooms
RATES	Single room with bath from
	280F to 300F
OPEN	February 15 to January 15
OWNER-MANAGER	Mr. and Mrs. R. Canac
AGENCY	Relais et Châteaux

Château de NIEUIL

ADDRESS	Château de Nieuil
	16270 Nieuil (Charente)
TELEPHONE	(45) 71 36 38
NUMBER OF ROOMS	10 rooms, 3 apartments
RATES	Single rooms from 280F to
	440F. Apartments from 450F to
	700F
OPEN	March 20 to November 15 and
	December 31 to January 10
OWNER-MANAGER	Michel Bodinaud

Château de Castel NOVEL

ADDRESS	Château de Castel Novel
	Route d'Objat
	19240 Varetz (Corrèze)
TELEPHONE	(55) 85 00 01
TELEX	590065
NUMBER OF ROOMS	23 rooms, 5 apartments

RATES	Single rooms from 300F to 390F. Apartments from 390F to 410F
OPEN	May 1 to October 24
OWNER-MANAGER	Albert Parveaux

Auberge de NOVES

ADDRESS	Auberge de Noves 13350 Noves (Bouches-du-Rhône)
TELEPHONE	(90) 94 19 21
TELEX	431312
NUMBER OF ROOMS	20 rooms, 2 apartments
RATES	Single room from 260F to 460F per person per night. Apartments from 300F to 700F per night
OPEN	Mid-February to January
OWNER-MANAGER	The Lalleman Family
AGENCY	Relais et Châteaux

Domaine de PERIGNY

ADDRESS	Domaine de Périgny 44400 Les Sorinières
TELEPHONE	(40) 54 70 25
TELEX	700610
NUMBER OF ROOMS	14 rooms, 3 apartments
RATES	Single room from 275F to 350F per person per night. Apartments from 360F to 450F
OPEN	Year-round
OWNER-MANAGER	M. Philippe Savry
AGENCY	Relais et Châteaux

Hôtel du PLATEAU DU ROY

	43
ADDRESS	Hôtel du Plateau du Roy
	Rieutord de Randon
	48700 Saint-Amans (Lozère)
TELEPHONE	(66) 47 33 03
NUMBER OF ROOMS	17 beds
RATES	Single room from 92F to 120F
OPEN	March 15 to November 15
OWNER-MANAGER	Guy Trauchessec

Château de PONDERACH

ADDRESS	Château de Ponderach
	Route de Narbonne
	34220 Saint-Pons (Herault)
TELEPHONE	(67) 97 02 57
NUMBER OF ROOMS	9 rooms
RATES	Single room from 280F to 300F
OPEN	Year-round
OWNER-MANAGER	Mr. and Mrs. Pierre Counotte
AGENCY	Relais et Châteaux

Hostellerie de la POSTE

ADDRESS	Hostellerie de la Poste
	13 Place Vauban
	89200 Avallon (Yonne)
TELEPHONE	(86) 34 06 12
NUMBER OF ROOMS	24 rooms, 6 apartments
RATES	Single room with breakfast from 350F to 420F. Apartments with bath and breakfast from 450F
OPEN	January through November
OWNER-MANAGER	Rene Hure
AGENCY	Relais et Châteaux

Les PRES D'EUGENIE

ADDRESS	Les Prés d'Eugenie
	40320 Eugénie-les-Bains
	(Landes)
TELEPHONE	(58) 58 19 01
TELEX	540470
NUMBER OF ROOMS	30 rooms, 6 apartments
RATES	Single room with bath from
	430F to 490F per person per
	night. Apartments from 600F to
	680F per night
OPEN	April 1 to November 1
OWNER-MANAGER	Michel and Christine Guerard
AGENCY	Relais et Châteaux

Le PRIEURE

A manor house dating back to the Renaissance.

ADDRESS	Le Prieuré
	Treves Cunaud
	49350 Chenehutte-les-Tuffeaux
	Gennes (Maine-et-Loire)
TELEPHONE	(41) 50 15 31
TELEX	720183
NUMBER OF ROOMS	36 rooms, 2 apartments
RATES	Single room with bath from
	160F to 425F. Apartments from
	350F to 525F
OPEN	March through December
OWNER-MANAGER	Rene Traversac and Philip
	Doumerc
AGENCY	Relais et Châteaux

Château de RIELL

ADDRESS	Château de Riell
	66500 Moltig-les-Bains
	(Pyrénées-Orientales)
TELEPHONE	(68) 96 20 56

TELEX	500705
NUMBER OF ROOMS	20 rooms, 2 apartments
RATES	Single room from 430F per person per night. Apartments from 604F per night
OPEN	March 1 to November 1
OWNER-MANAGER	Biche Barthelemy
AGENCY	Relais et Châteaux

Château de ROCHEGUDE

Located on a rocky bluff from which the chateau and the surrounding village got its name, the Chateau de Rochegude was once a fortified stronghold against the Huguenots in the sixteenth

century. Reconstructed and partly rebuilt in the seventeenth century, the chateau features a dungeon in the middle of the main quadrangle. The terraces date back to the eighteenth century, and there are several vaulted chambers, an eighteenth century staircase and underground cellars excavated from the primeval rock.

ADDRESS	Château de Rochegude 26130 Rochegude (Drôme)
TELEPHONE	(75) 04 81 88
TELEX	345661
NUMBER OF ROOMS	25 rooms, 4 apartments and suites
RATES	Single room with bath from 180F. Double room with bath from 210F to 600F. Suites from 800F to 1,000F per night
OPEN	Year-round except October 1 to March 1
OWNER-MANAGER	Mr. and Mrs. Gailbert and A. Chabert
AGENCY	Relais et Châteaux

Château de ROUMEGOUSE

The site of the chateau, dating back to the tenth century, was once owned by the Episcopal Church of Cahors. Later sold to the Lord of Castelneau, it was converted into a military stronghold. Destroyed during the battles over the years, the chateau was purchased near the end of the nineteenth century and rebuilt as seen today. The interior was completely renovated and redecorated about fifteen years ago, and the chateau was converted into a hotel.

ADDRESS	Château de Roumégouse 46500 Rignac (Aveyron)
TELEPHONE	(65) 33 63 81
RATES	Room with bath from 190F to 265F. Apartments from 320F to 450F
OPEN	April 1 to November 2
OWNER-MANAGER	The Lauwaert and Laine Families
AGENCY	Relais et Châteaux

Hostellerie SAINTE-CATHERINE

ADDRESS	Hostellerie Sainte-Catherine
	16220 Montbron-Agnouléme
	(Charente)
TELEPHONE	(45) 70 60 03
NUMBER OF ROOMS	12 beds
RATES	Single room with breakfast
	from 100F to 120F
OPEN	Year-round
OWNER-MANAGER	A. Qu'hen
AGENCY	Relais du Silence

Château SAINT-JACQUES

An eighteenth-century French chateau located about a ninety-minute drive from Paris near the Yonne River.

ADDRESS	Château Saint-Jacques
	14 Faubourg de Paris
	89300 Joigny (Yonne)
TELEPHONE	(86) 62 09 70
NUMBER OF ROOMS	18 rooms
OPEN	February through November
OWNER-MANAGER	Jacqueline and Michel Lorain

Château SAINT-JEAN

An old castle dating back to the days of the Knights of Malta during the twelfth century. Located in a private park, the chapel has been converted into a dining room.

ADDRESS	Château Saint-Jean
	Parc St.-Jean
	03100 Montlucon (Allier)
TELEPHONE	(70) 05 04 65
NUMBER OF ROOMS	8 rooms with bath or shower

RATES	Single room with bath from 160F to 350F
OPEN	Year-round
OWNER-MANAGER	Odile Brock

Château SAINT-MARTIN

ADDRESS	Château Saint-Martin Route de Coursegoules 06140 Vence (Alpes-Maritime)
TELEPHONE	(93) 58 02 02
TELEX	470282
NUMBER OF ROOMS	16 rooms in the chateau, 10 apartments and villas
RATES	Single room from 450F to 950F per person per night. Apartments from 500F per night
OPEN	March through November
OWNER-MANAGER	The Geneve Family and Andree Brunet
AGENCY	Relais et Châteaux

Château de la SALLE

ADDRESS	Château de la Salle 5021 Montpinchon (Manche)
TELEPHONE	(33) 46 95 19
NUMBER OF ROOMS	10 rooms
RATES	Single rooms from 260F to 350F per person per night
OPEN	March 28 to November 2
OWNER-MANAGER	Mr. and Mrs. Lemesle

Château du SCIPIONNET

ADDRESS	Château du Scipionnèt 07140 Les Vans (Ardèche)
TELEPHONE	(75) 37 23 84
NUMBER OF ROOMS	23 beds

RATES   Single room from 40F to 150F
                per person per night
OPEN   March 30 to September 30
OWNER-MANAGER   J. Didier
AGENCY   Relais du Silence

Manoir du STANG

ADDRESS   Manoir du Stang
                29133 La Forêt-Fouesnant
                  (Finistere)
TELEPHONE   (98) 56 02 22
RATES   Single room with bath and two
                meals from 540F to 600F per
                person per day
OPEN   Year-round
OWNER-MANAGER   Guy Hubert

Château de TEILDRAS

ADDRESS   Château de Teildras
                49330 Cheffes
TELEPHONE   (41) 42 61 08
TELEX   720910
NUMBER OF ROOMS 9 rooms
RATES   Single room from 300F to 460F
                per person per night
OPEN   March 1 to November 15
OWNER-MANAGER   Count and Countess de Ber-
                nard du Breil
AGENCY   Relais et Châteaux

Auberge des TEMPLIERS

ADDRESS   Auberge des Templiers
                Boismorand
                45290 Les Bezards
TELEPHONE   (38) 31 80 01
TELEX   780998

NUMBER OF ROOMS	20 rooms, 7 apartments
RATES	Single room with bath from 230F to 520F. Apartments from 520F to 920F per night
OPEN	Mid-February to mid-January
OWNER-MANAGER	Philipe and M. J. Depee
AGENCY	Relais et Châteaux

Le Domaine de la TORTINIERE

The history of la Tortinière and the surrounding area dates back to the days of the Roman period. The path leading from the entrance to the park following the walls of the property along the river is called the "white lane," perhaps because of the chalky stones that were used to construct the walkway. At the end of the tenth century, the Donjon of Montbazon was built by Foulques Norra (the Black Falcon), and between 991 and 997 he built numerous fortresses in the area. In 1040 the castle of Montbazon became the property of Philippe Savary, and in 1459 King Charles VII lived here. The present chateau was built around 1861 in the Renaissance style. In 1923 the estate was sold for 600,000 old francs, and it was converted into a hotel in 1955.

ADDRESS	Le Domaine de la Tortinière 37250 Montbazon-en-Touraine (Indre-et-Loire)
TELEPHONE	(47) 26 00 19
TELEX	750806
NUMBER OF ROOMS	21 rooms, 11 in the chateau, 10 in three pavilions
RATES	Twin room with bath from 440F. Double room with bath from 375F. Suites with bath from 565F
OPEN	Year-round
OWNER-MANAGER	Madame D. Olivereau-Capron

Château des TOUCHES

ADDRESS	Château des Touches 79110 La Boudranche-Gournay (Deux-Sévres)

TELEPHONE	(49) 27 04 29
NUMBER OF ROOMS	15 beds
RATES	Single room from 110F to 240F
OPEN	February 28 to January 2
OWNER-MANAGER	Chef Boutonne
AGENCY	Relais du Silence

La TOUR DE PACORET

ADDRESS	La Tour de Pacoret
	73740 Grésy-sur-Isère (Savoie)
TELEPHONE	(79) 32 44 12
NUMBER OF ROOMS	12 beds
RATES	Single room from 50F to 90F
OPEN	January 15 to October 15
OWNER-MANAGER	Miles Vellat

La Bastide de TOURTOUR

ADDRESS	La Bastide de Tourtour
	83690 Tourtour, Salernes (Var)
TELEPHONE	(94) 70 57 30
NUMBER OF ROOMS	26 rooms
RATES	Single room with bath from 250F to 600F
OPEN	March 20 to November 12
OWNER-MANAGER	Mr. and Mrs. Laurent

Château de TRIGANCE

A sixteenth-century chateau fortress.

ADDRESS	Château de Trigance
	83840 Trigance (Var)
TELEPHONE	(94) 76 91 18
NUMBER OF ROOMS	7 rooms and 1 apartment
RATES	Single room from 120F to 290F. Apartments from 340F
OPEN	March through November
OWNER-MANAGER	Mr. and Mrs. Thomas
AGENCY	Relais et Châteaux

Château des TROIS POETES

A sixteenth-century chateau located near the Pyrenees on private parklands.

ADDRESS	Château des Trois Poètes
	64300 Castetis-par-Orthez
	(Pyrénées-Atlantiques)
TELEPHONE	(59) 69 16 20
NUMBER OF ROOMS	10 rooms
RATES	Single room from 65F to 120F
OPEN	March 1 to November 30
OWNER-MANAGER	Mr. and Mrs. Simonet

Le VIEUX CASTILLON

ADDRESS	Le Vieux Castillon
	Castillon-du-Gard
	30210 Remoulins (Gard)
TELEPHONE	(66) 37 00 77
NUMBER OF ROOMS	21 rooms, 2 apartments
RATES	Single rooms with breakfast (no bath) from 220F to 450F per person per night. Apartments from 575F to 735F per night
OPEN	March 13 to January 10
OWNER-MANAGER	R. Traversac

Ostellerie du VIEUX PEROUGES

A historic hotel dating back to the thirteenth century with rooms furnished in fifteenth- and sixteenth-century antiques.

ADDRESS	Ostellerie du Vieux Pérouges
	87350 Panazol (Ain)
TELEPHONE	(74) 61 00 88
RATES	Rooms from 400F per night
OPEN	Year-round
OWNER-MANAGER	Georges Thibaut

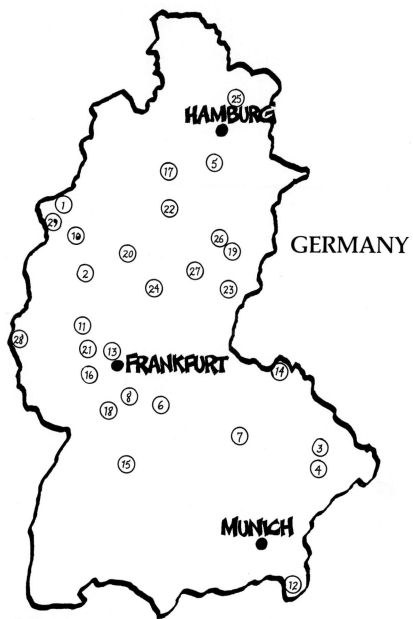

1. Parkhotel Wasserburg Anholt
2. Schloss Auel
3. Schlosshotel Egg
4. Burg Falkenfels
5. Fürstenhof Celle
6. Burghotel Götzenburg
7. Greifen-Post
8. Schlosshotel auf Burg Hirschhorn
9. Schlosshotel Hochhausen
10. Schloss Hugenpoet
11. Hotel Klostergut Jakobsberg
12. Könligliche Villa
13. Schlosshotel Kronberg
14. Burghotel Laurenstein
15. Schlosshotel Monrepos
16. Hotel Jagdschloss Niederwald
17. Schloss Petershagen
18. Zum Ritter
19. Burghotel Sababurg
20. Burghotel Schnellenberg
21. Burghotel auf Schönburg
22. Schlosshotel Burg Schwalenberg
23. Schloss Spangenberg
24. Hotel Stadtpalais
25. Hotel Schloss Tremsbüttel
26. Burg Trendelburg
27. Burghotel Schloss Waldeck
28. Hotel Burg Winnenthal
29. Hotel Schloss Zell

CONTENTS

Parkhotel Wasserburg ANHOLT

A breath of Versailles in northern Germany near the Netherland border, the Wasserburg Anholt is a beautiful moated castle surrounded by parks, a deer refuge, and a golf course. The large towers date back to Roman times when they were used as a refuge by residents. Pile gratings used as the foundation of the castle and stones found in the lower walls indicate that the towers were built around the twelfth century and the remaining structures during the thirteenth and fourteenth centuries. The Thirty Years' War showed that ancient structures like this were no match for modern fire-power, so the castle was converted into a private residence at the turn of the seventeenth century.

ADDRESS	Parkhotel Wasserburg Anholt
Kleverstrasse
4294 Anholt (Westfalen)
TELEPHONE	(02874) 20 44
NUMBER OF ROOMS	10 double rooms, 5 single rooms
RATES	Single room with two meals daily from 70DM to 135DM per person per day
OPEN	Year-round except February
OWNER-MANAGER	Heinz Brune
AGENCY	Gast im Schloss

Schloss AUEL

This hotel once hosted Napoleon and features a Baroque chapel, indoor swimming pool, and rooms furnished in period antiques.

ADDRESS	Schloss Auel
	5204 Lohmar 21 (Wahlscheid)
TELEPHONE	(02206) 20 41
TELEX	887510
NUMBER OF ROOMS	4 single rooms, 19 double rooms
RATES	Single rooms from 70DM to 95DM per person per night. Double room from 100DM to 155DM per night
OPEN	Year-round
OWNER-MANAGER	The Baron and Baroness v. la Vallette St. Georges
AGENCY	Gast im Schloss

Schlosshotel EGG

Built as a fortified castle in the 1100s, Schloss Egg was converted in 1830, and the historic outhouses have been transformed into a hotel and restaurant with apartments furnished in period antiques and four-poster beds. The restaurant is located in what was once the royal stable, and weddings are held regularly in the castle's wedding chapel.

ADDRESS	Schlosshotel Egg
	8351 Egg bei Deggendorf
TELEPHONE	(09905) 2 89
RATES	Single rooms from 60DM, double rooms from 90DM for two
OPEN	Year-round except November
OWNER-MANAGER	Gl.L. Hartl and C. Fellner
AGENCY	Gast im Schloss

Burg FALKENFELS

ADDRESS	Burg Falkenfels
	8441 Falkenfels über Straubing
TELEPHONE	(09961) 63 85
OPEN	Year-round

FÜRSTENHOF CELLE

A Baroque seventeenth-century mansion completely restored to its original style. All rooms have private bath and are furnished with seventeenth- and eighteenth-century antiques.

ADDRESS	Fürstenhof Celle
	Hannoverstrasse 5–56
	3100 Celle
TELEPHONE	(05141) 2 70 5
TELEX	925293
NUMBER OF ROOMS	26 single rooms, 36 double rooms
RATES	Single rooms from 83DM to 137DM, double rooms from 110DM to 180DM
OPEN	Year-round
OWNER-MANAGER	H. Bruhl
AGENCY	Gast im Schloss, Relais et Châteaux

Burghotel GÖTZENBURG

The birthplace of Gotz von Berlichingen in the year 1480, the Gotzenburg features a castle museum, elegantly furnished rooms, bowling alley, and shooting ranges.

ADDRESS	Burghotel Götzenburg
	7109 Jagsthausen
TELEPHONE	(07943) 22 22
NUMBER OF ROOMS	5 single rooms, 9 double rooms
RATES	Single rooms from 45DM to 50DM. Double rooms from 65DM to 80DM

OPEN	March 16 to November 15
OWNER-MANAGER	Baron von Berlichingen and J. Bircks
AGENCY	Gast im Schloss

GREIFEN-POST

Dating back to the year 1588, the Greifen-Post has been owned by the same family for four generations. Located within driving distance of Nuremberg and Würzburg, the hotel specializes in Franconian cuisine.

ADDRESS	Greifen-Post Marktplatz 7 8805 Feuchtwangen
TELEPHONE	(09852) 20 02
NUMBER OF ROOMS	37 rooms with bath or shower, 8 rooms without
RATES	Single rooms from 38DM to 68DM. Double rooms from 60DM to 120DM per night
OPEN	Year-round
OWNER-MANAGER	E. Lorentz
AGENCY	Romantik Hotels

Schlosshotel auf Burg HIRSCHHORN

Since the twelfth century, this castle hotel has towered over the Neckar Valley, acting as a fortress against invaders.

ADDRESS	Schlosshotel auf Burg Hirschhorn 6932 Hirschhorn/Neckar
TELEPHONE	(06272) 13 73
NUMBER OF ROOMS	6 single rooms, 9 double rooms
RATES	Single rooms from 28DM. Double rooms from 56DM to 135DM
OPEN	February 15 to January 2
OWNER-MANAGER	H. Henkel
AGENCY	Gast im Schloss

Schlosshotel HOCHHAUSEN

Of early medieval construction, this hotel was rebuilt in the Baroque style of architecture in 1753. Opened as a guest house in 1954, it's been in the hands of the same family for over three hundred years.

ADDRESS	Schlosshotel Hochhausen
	6954 Hassmersheim-Hoch-
	hausen
TELEPHONE	(06261) 31 42
NUMBER OF ROOMS	4 single rooms, 7 double rooms
RATES	Single rooms from 30DM to
	37DM. Double rooms from
	60DM to 75DM
OPEN	Year-round
OWNER-MANAGER	The Riederer-Helmstaff Families
AGENCY	Gast im Schloss

Schloss HUGENPOET

Schloss Hugenpoet is a sixteenth-century moated castle hotel located in a sprawling parklands between Essen and Dusseldorf. The hotel features old fireplaces, antique furnishings in all rooms, and a private art collection.

ADDRESS	Schloss Hugenpoet
	August-Thyssenstrasse 51
	4300 Essen 18 (Kettwig)
TELEPHONE	(02054) 60 54
NUMBER OF ROOMS	8 single rooms, 15 double
	rooms
RATES	Single rooms from 60DM to
	120DM per person per night.
	Double rooms from 150DM to
	180DM per night
OPEN	Year-round
OWNER-MANAGER	J. Naumann
AGENCY	Gast im Schloss, Relais et
	Châteaux

Hotel KLOSTERGUT JAKOBSBERG

A former monastery, founded in 1157 by Barbarossa, the Hotel Jakobsberg sits on a hill overlooking the Rhine River on a wildlife park. It features an indoor swimming pool, bowling alley, and chapel.

ADDRESS	Hotel Klostergut Jakobsberg
	5407 Boppard/Rhein
TELEPHONE	(06742) 30 21
TELEX	426323
NUMBER OF ROOMS	4 single rooms, 104 double rooms
RATES	Single room with bath from 50DM to 105DM. Double room from 70DM to 160DM
OPEN	Year-round
OWNER-MANAGER	J. Zastrow
AGENCY	Gast im Schloss

KÖNIGLICHE VILLA

Built in 1848, the villa served as the summer residence of the Bavarian kings until 1918 when it was converted into a hotel. Tastefully renovated with all of the modern conveniences, it has its own wine cellar, a specialty restaurant, and indoor swimming pool.

ADDRESS	Königliche Villa
	Am Luitpoldpark
	8240 Berchtesgaden
TELEPHONE	(08652) 50 97
NUMBER OF ROOMS	8 single rooms, 27 double rooms
RATES	Single rooms from 50DM to 70DM. Double rooms from 90DM to 120DM
OPEN	Year-round
OWNER-MANAGER	Lorenz Family
AGENCY	Gast im Schloss

Schlosshotel KRONBERG

ADDRESS	Schlosshotel Kronberg
	Hainstrasse 25
	6242 Kronberg/Taunus
TELEPHONE	(016173) 70 11
TELEX	415424
NUMBER OF ROOMS	53 rooms, 2 apartments
RATES	Single room with bath from 220DM to 265DM per person per night. Apartments from 350DM to 565DM per night
OPEN	Year-round
OWNER-MANAGER	Klaus Fischer
AGENCY	Relais et Châteaux

Burghotel LAUENSTEIN

ADDRESS	Burghotel Lauenstein
	Burgstrasse 4
	8642 Lauenstein
TELEPHONE	(09263) 2 56
RATES	Single room with bath from 32DM per person per night. Rooms with two meals from 39DM to 50DM per person per day. Rooms with all meals from 45DM to 55DM per day
OPEN	Closed February
OWNER-MANAGER	The Wagner Family

Schlosshotel MONREPOS

ADDRESS	Schlosshotel Monrepos
	7140 Ludwigsburg bei Stuttgart
TELEPHONE	(07141) 301 01
TELEX	7264720
NUMBER OF ROOMS	83 rooms, 2 apartments

RATES	Single room from 118DM to 185DM per person per night. Apartments from 260DM per night
OPEN	Year-round
OWNER-MANAGER	Gisela Gruber and H. Tonk
AGENCY	Relais et Châteaux

Hotel Jagdschloss NIEDERWALD

This hotel was once the hunting castle of the Counts of Stein and the Duke of Nassau. Between 1723 and 1729 the main building was constructed, and since the middle of the nineteenth century the estate has been owned by the government in Hessen.

In 1977, Egon Dirschinger leased the hotel and has added his personal touch to this unique establishment.

ADDRESS	Hotel Jagdschloss Niederwald 6220 Rüdesheim am Rhein
TELEPHONE	(06722) 10 04
TELEX	42152
RATES	Single rooms with breakfast from 75DM to 95DM. Double rooms with breakfast from 140DM to 160DM. Suites from 120DM to 135DM
OPEN	Year-round
OWNER-MANAGER	Egon Dirschinger
AGENCY	Gast im Schloss

Schloss PETERSHAGEN

This former palace of the Prince Bishops dates back to the year 1306 and is located on the banks of the Weser River.

| ADDRESS | Schloss Petershagen 4953 Petershagen an der Weser |
| TELEPHONE | (05707) 3 46 |

NUMBER OF ROOMS	2 single rooms, 5 double rooms
RATES	Single rooms from 50DM to 70DM. Double rooms from 90DM to 120DM
OPEN	March 1 to January 10
OWNER-MANAGER	K. Hestermann
AGENCY	Gast im Schloss

Zum RITTER

This hotel was built in the year 1592 and is located near Heidelberg's city center.

ADDRESS	Zum Ritter Hauptstrasse 178 6900 Heidelberg
TELEPHONE	(06221) 2 42 72
TELEX	0461506
NUMBER OF ROOMS	27 rooms with bath or shower, 9 rooms without
RATES	Single room from 45DM to 80DM per person per night. Double rooms from 75DM to 170DM per night
OPEN	Year-round
OWNER-MANAGER	G. Kuchelmeister
AGENCY	Romantik Hotels

Burghotel SABABURG

Sababurg, the Sleeping Beauty Castle of the Brothers Grimm fairy tale, was founded in 1334 and features tower rooms and spacious terraces surrounded by a nature preservation park.

ADDRESS	Burghotel Sababurg 3520 Hofgeismar-Sababurg 5
TELEPHONE	(05678) 10 52
NUMBER OF ROOMS	2 single rooms, 13 double rooms
RATES	Single rooms from 38DM to 48DM, double rooms from 65DM to 120DM

OPEN	March 28 to January 3
OWNER-MANAGER	K. Koseck
AGENCY	Gast im Schloss

Burghotel SCHNELLENBERG

First mentioned in the year 1225, this fortress sits on a hill in Westfalia, within an hour's drive from Frankfurt and the Ruhr areas. Surrounded by woods, the hotel features tower apartments, a museum, a Knight's Hall, and a chapel.

ADDRESS	Burghotel Schnellenberg 5952 Attendorn im Sauer- land
TELEPHONE	(02722) 40 81
TELEX	876732
NUMBER OF ROOMS	10 single rooms, 36 double rooms
RATES	Single rooms from 55DM to 80DM per person per night. Double rooms from 90DM to 140DM per night
OPEN	February 5 to January 5
OWNER-MANAGER	The Bilsing Family
AGENCY	Gast im Schloss

Burghotel auf SCHÖNBURG

The Burghotel auf Schonburg sits high over the Rhine River, a small historic hotel in a romantic European setting. The hotel dates back over a thousand years and features narrow passages leading to secret chambers. From the hotel's terrace, there's a fantastic view of the countryside and a nearby yacht harbor. Victor Hugo once described this castle hotel as one of the most venerable hills of rubble in all of Europe. Built on towering rocks overlooking the Rhine Valley and the Enge-Holler Gorge, the castle was partially destroyed during a seventeenth-century battle, then completely rebuilt.

ADDRESS	Burghotel auf Schönburg 6532 Oberwesel am Rhein

TELEPHONE	(06744) 81 98
TELEX	042300
NUMBER OF ROOMS	10 double rooms
RATES	Single rooms from 65DM to 103DM per person per night. Room with two meals from 75DM per person per day
OPEN	Year-round except January
OWNER-MANAGER	H. Huttl
AGENCY	Gast im Schloss

Schlosshotel Burg SCHWALENBERG

Founded in 1231, the Schwalenberg Castle features rooms furnished in royal elegance, an outdoor restaurant, and a commanding view of the Lipper Valley.

ADDRESS	Schlosshotel Burg Schwal-enberg 3284 Schieder-Schwalenberg
TELEPHONE	(05284) 51 67
NUMBER OF ROOMS	18 rooms
RATES	Single rooms with bath from 70DM, double rooms with bath from 65DM to 130DM per person per night
OPEN	January 31 to January 10
OWNER-MANAGER	The Saul Family
AGENCY	Gast im Schloss

Schloss SPANGENBERG

First mentioned in local history in the year 1214, this castle towers over the city of the same name. It has a Knight's Hall, excellent restaurant with wine cellar, and its own museum. Surrounded by a moat with towering walls and turrets, it's located between Frankfurt and Hanover.

ADDRESS	Schloss Spangenberg 3509 Spangenberg
TELEPHONE	(05663) 8 66

NUMBER OF ROOMS	23 rooms
RATES	Single room without bath from 55DM to 65DM per person per night. Double room from 80DM to 125DM
OPEN	March through January
OWNER-MANAGER	J. Erschens
AGENCY	Gast im Schloss

Hotel STADTPALAIS

This late Gothic mansion, built in the old Hanseatic town of Lemgo, was restored in 1540 in the original Weser Renaissance style. All of the rooms are furnished with period antiques, and the hotel's gourmet restaurant specializes in French cuisine.

ADDRESS	Hotel Stadtpalais Papenstrasse 24 4920 Lemgo
TELEPHONE	(05261) 1 04 81
NUMBER OF ROOMS	3 single rooms, 10 double rooms
RATES	Single rooms from 55DM. Double rooms from 95DM to 110DM
OPEN	Year-round
OWNER-MANAGER	W. Brinkman
AGENCY	Gast im Schloss

Hotel Schloss TREMSBÜTTEL

The Wedding Castle of Germany, Tremsbüttel lies on the outskirts of Hamburg and features elegantly furnished rooms and gourmet dining.

ADDRESS	Hotel Schloss Tremsbüttel Schlosstrasse 6 2017 Tremsbüttel (Holstein)
TELEPHONE	(04532) 65 44
NUMBER OF ROOMS	4 single rooms, 16 double rooms

RATES	Single room from 68DM to 73DM. Double room from 95DM to 175DM
OPEN	Year-round
OWNER-MANAGER	H. W. May
AGENCY	Gast im Schloss

Burg TRENDELBURG

The Burg Trendelburg is a medieval castle located by the Forest of Reinhard north of Frankfort. A room in the wedding tower features antique furnishings and a four-poster bed.

ADDRESS	Burg Trendelburg 3526 Trendelburg 1 (Kreis Hofgeismar)
TELEPHONE	(05675) 10 21
TELEX	994812
NUMBER OF ROOMS	5 single rooms, 18 double rooms
RATES	Single rooms from 50DM to 70DM per person per night. Double room from 90DM to 140DM per night
OPEN	February through November
OWNER-MANAGER	The Stockhausen Family
AGENCY	Gast im Schloss

Burghotel Schloss WALDECK

Schloss Waldeck is located on the edge of Germany's highest reservoir near the Edersee.

ADDRESS	Burghotel Schloss Waldeck 3544 Waldeck am Edersee
TELEPHONE	(05623) 53 24
NUMBER OF ROOMS	4 single rooms, 11 double rooms
RATES	Single rooms from 50DM to 65DM. Double rooms from 90DM to 110DM

OPEN	March 15 to November 1
OWNER-MANAGER	K. F. Isenberg
AGENCY	Gast im Schloss

Hotel Burg WINNENTHAL

Located four miles from the old Roman city of Xanten, the Hotel Winnenthal is the oldest moated castle in the Lower Rhine area. Within the walls of the castle, there's a modern farm, a distillery, and an excellent hotel featuring international cuisine.

ADDRESS	Hotel Burg Winnenthal 4232 Xanten-Winnenthal
TELEPHONE	(02802) 30 37
TELEX	812707
NUMBER OF ROOMS	12 single rooms, 24 double rooms
RATES	Single rooms from 50DM to 60DM. Double rooms from 100DM to 120DM
OPEN	Year-round
OWNER-MANAGER	F. K. Schmitz-Winnenthal
AGENCY	Gast im Schloss

Hotel Schloss ZELL

Located in the Mosel Valley, about fifty miles from Koblenz and Trier, this 750-year-old Gothic castle has its own vineyards, tower rooms furnished in period antiques, and a swimming pool.

ADDRESS	Hotel Schloss Zell Schlosstrasse 8 5583 Zell/Mosel
TELEPHONE	(06542) 40 84
NUMBER OF ROOMS	3 single rooms, 3 double rooms
RATES	Single rooms from 40DM to 65DM per person per night. Double rooms from 90DM to 160DM per night
OPEN	January 31 to December 1
OWNER-MANAGER	J. Bohn
AGENCY	Gast im Schloss

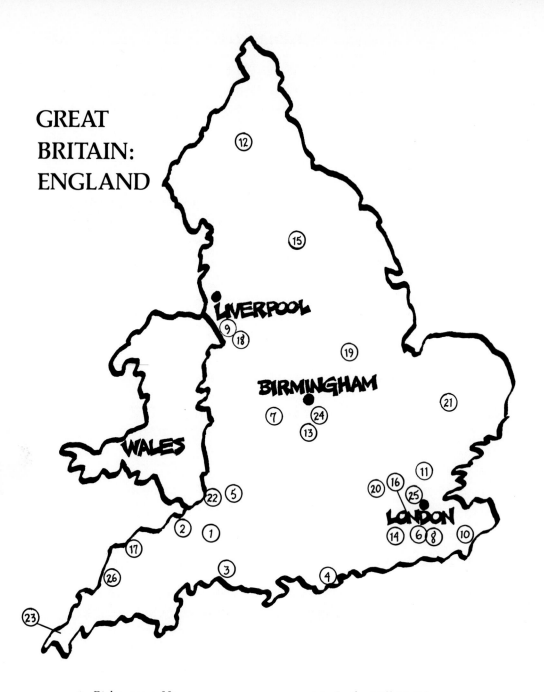

GREAT
BRITAIN:
ENGLAND

1. Bishoptrow House
2. The Castle Hotel
3. Chedington Court
4. Chewton Glen Hotel
5. The Close at Tetbury
6. The Copthorne Hotel
7. The Elms
8. Gravetye Manor
9. Hunter's Lodge
10. Hotel Imperial
11. Letchworth Hall
12. The Lord Crewe Arms
13. Lygon Arms

14. Lythe Hill Hotel
15. The Old Swan Hotel
16. Pennyhill Park Hotel
17. Portledge Hotel
18. Rookery Hall
19. Rothley Court
20. Studley Priory Hotel
21. Swynford Paddocks
22. Thornbury Castle Restaurant
23. Tregenna Castle Hotel
24. Welcombe Hotel
25. West Lodge Park Hotel
26. Woodford Bridge Hotel

CONTENTS

BISHOPTROW HOUSE

ADDRESS	Bishoptrow House
	Warminster, Siltshire
	VA129 HH
TELEPHONE	(0985) 212.312
NUMBER OF ROOMS	9 single rooms, 1 apartment
RATES	Single rooms from £42 to £58 per person per night. Apartments from £58 per night
OPEN	Mid-March to November
OWNER-MANAGER	Jenny Jukes
AGENCY	Relais et Châteaux

The CASTLE Hotel

Taunton Castle, with which the hotel is closely connected, is the earliest English fortress in England's written historical records. Built in 710 A.D. by the King of Wessex, the castle was burned down in 722 and later became the residence of the Bishops of Winchester. The castle was rebuilt in 1495 and was captured in battle in 1497.

Much of the hotel as it exists today is medieval in style. Some of the bedrooms stand on the old gateway and were probably rebuilt by bishops around the end of the eighteenth century. During the eighteenth and nineteenth centuries, the hotel provided luxury accommodations for travelers along the King's Highway. Former guests include Queen Victoria, the Duchess of Kent, King Edward VII and VIII, and Queen Elizabeth.

The walls on one side of the estate once formed part of a building dating back to the 1300s. Two glass frames have been attached to these walls and the plaster removed, so that the ancient brickwork can be seen. The archway, under the south wing of the hotel and over the old main road between London and Plymouth, was originally the eastern gate, built about 1300 and restored in 1495. The grooves in which the portcullis was raised and lowered are still visible, as are the original hinge hooks of the main gates where the drawbridge and outer moat were located.

ADDRESS	The Castle Hotel
	Castle Green, Taunton
	Somerset TA1 1NF
TELEPHONE	(0823) 726.71
TELEX	46488
RATES	Double or twin room with bath
	from £49 to £59 per night.
	Single room with bath from
	£31 per person per night
OWNER-MANAGER	C.H.G. Chapman
AGENCY	Prestige Hotels

CHEDINGTON COURT

Chedington Court is a Jacobean-style manor hour located on four hundred acres surrounded by gardens and sweeping lawns.

ADDRESS	Chedington Court
	Chedington, Beaminster
	Dorset DT8 3HY
TELEPHONE	(093598) 265
NUMBER OF ROOMS	16 beds in 8 rooms with bath
	or shower
RATES	Single rooms from £18.50 to
	£25.85 per person per night.
	Double rooms from £30.80 to
	£46.20 per night
OPEN	Year-round
OWNER-MANAGER	Hilary and Philip Chapman
AGENCY	Romantik Hotels

CHEWTON GLEN Hotel

Chewton Glen is a stately mansion house set on thirty acres of parkland along the edge of the New Forest, about a half mile off the coast of the English Channel.

ADDRESS	Chewton Glen Hotel
	New Milton
	Hampshire BH25 6QS
TELEPHONE	Highcliffe (04252) 53.41
TELEX	41456

NUMBER OF ROOMS	45 rooms with bath, 7 suites
OPEN	Year-round
OWNER-MANAGER	David Brockett
AGENCIES	Prestige Hotels, Relais et Châteaux

The CLOSE AT TETBURY

The Close at Tetbury is a beautiful example of the traditional English country mansion. Originally the home of a prosperous wool merchant, it was built around the end of the seventeenth century on the site of a Cistercian monastery. The hotel's restaurant faces south into a walled garden filled with lime trees.

ADDRESS	The Close At Tetbury
	8 Long Street
	Tetbury, Gloucestershire
	GL8 8AQ
TELEPHONE	(0666) 522.72
NUMBER OF ROOMS	12 4ooms with bath
OPEN	Year-round
OWNER-MANAGER	J. M. Lauzier and M. R. Weston
AGENCY	Prestige Hotels

The COPTHORNE Hotel

This hotel is set around a sixteenth-century farmhouse on one hundred acres of gardens, glades, and woodlands. It's located five minutes from Gatwick airport by train, near the former home of Sir Winston Churchill.

ADDRESS	The Copthorne Hotel
	Copthorne
	Crawley, Sussex
TELEPHONE	Copthorne 714.971
TELEX	95500
NUMBER OF ROOMS	221 rooms with bath, 9 suites
OPEN	Year-round
OWNER-MANAGER	M. C. Bryant

The ELMS

The Elms was built in 1710 during the reign of Queen Anne by architect Gilbert White. As far back as the estate's records go, the house has always been known as The Elms. In 1840, the house became part of the Abberly Hall estate, and in 1916 it was leased by Sir Richard Brook-Baroney, a well-known English racehorse breeder. When Sir Richard purchased the estate, he added wings and massive fireplaces and installed the doorways from his family's home, Norton Priory in Cheshire. When construction was completed, the Elms caught fire and was completely gutted, with only the main walls remaining. Sir Richard rebuilt the house and lived there until 1946, when the property was sold and turned into a hotel.

ADDRESS   The Elms
                                 Abberley near Worcester
                                 WR6 6AT

TELEPHONE	Great Witley (029 921) 666
TELEX	337105
NUMBER OF ROOMS	20 bedrooms with bath
OPEN	Year-round
OWNER-MANAGER	Donald Crosthwaite and Rita Mooney
AGENCY	Prestige Hotels

GRAVETYE MANOR

Gravetye Manor was built in 1598 by Richard Infield for his bride, Katharine Compton. The initials "R" and "K" can still be seen in the stone over the main entrance door off the formal gardens, and the portraits of the previous owners are carved in oak over the fireplace in the master bedroom. At one time, the manor house was used as a smuggler's hideout and store. William Robinson, one of England's most famous gardeners, purchased the estate and one thousand acres of land in 1884 and lived there until he died in 1935. Robinson created an elaborate formal garden in a style which is now copied around the world. In remodeling the manor, he paneled the interior of the house in wood from the estate.

The manor house has been a hotel since 1958. The bedrooms are named after trees on the estate.

ADDRESS	Gravetye Manor
	East Grimstead
	West Sussex RH19 4LJ
TELEPHONE	(0342) 81.05.67
TELEX	957239
NUMBER OF ROOMS	14 rooms
RATES	Single room from £36 to £70
	per person per night
OPEN	Year-round
OWNER-MANAGER	Peter Herbert and Helmut
	Kircher
AGENCY	Relais et Châteaux

HUNTER'S LODGE

Hunter's Lodge is a period hotel built in 1671. Situated on five acres of country grounds, it's located about an hour's drive from Manchester.

ADDRESS	Hunter's Lodge
	Broxton, Cheshire

TELEPHONE	Broxton 982.925
NUMBER OF ROOMS	11 rooms with bath
RATES	Single rooms with bath and breakfast from £12.50 per person per night (winter) to £22 per person (summer). Double room with bath and breakfast from £17.50 to £24 per person per night
OPEN	Year-round
OWNER-MANAGER	Mr. and Mrs. S. A. Fennessey

Hotel IMPERIAL

The Hotel Imperial is a one-hundred-year-old manor house on fifty-two acres of private gardens and parklands stretching along the edge of the English Channel in southeastern England. The Imperial is considered to be one of the premier hotels in this area of England and is ideally situated for day excursions into Canterbury, Kent, and Rye.

ADDRESS	Hotel Imperial Princes Parade Hythe, Kent CT21 6AE
TELEPHONE	(0303) 674.41
NUMBER OF ROOMS	72 bedrooms, 68 with bath, 2 suites
OPEN	Year-round
OWNER-MANAGER	Christopher Beaven
AGENCY	Prestige Hotels

LETCHWORTH HALL

Letchworth is an early seventeenth-century manor house standing on the site of a building that was mentioned in local history as early as the twelfth century. Originally a Saxon homestead, the hotel dates back to the days of the Norman conquest when the estate was granted by William the Conqueror to Robert Gernon, a Norman baron. In the early twelfth century the estate, with its twelve acres of land, was willed to the Monastery of St. Albans and remained in church hands until the reign of Edward I.

The original building was destroyed by fire, and a moated

mansion was built on the site. In 1536 the estate became the property of Thomas Snagge, who went on to become the Attorney General of Ireland. Between 1620 and 1624 the present building was built, then sold for $22,000. Additions were added in 1846, and in the early 1900s Letchworth opened its doors as a hotel.

ADDRESS	Letchworth Hall Letchworth Hertfordshire SG6 3NP
TELEPHONE	Letchworth 3747
NUMBER OF ROOMS	48 rooms
RATES	Single room with bath and breakfast from £13 per person per night (weekends) to £23 per person per night (weekdays). Double room with bath and breakfast from £23 to £36.50 per night per person. Executive suites from £60 to £71.30 per night
OPEN	Year-round
OWNER-MANAGER	R. Pavedona

The LORD CREWE ARMS

The Lord Crewe Arms is located in the middle of the village of Blanchland in the Northumbrian countryside, about thirty miles from Newcastle-Upon-Tyne. In 1704, the village was purchased by Lord Crewe and upon his death in 1721, the estate was placed in trust. A complete village restoration program began in 1750, and the town appears today much as it did over two hundred years ago. It's said that the ghost of a former resident, Dorothy Foster, walks the halls of the hotel at night.

ADDRESS	Lord Crewe Arms Blanchland near Consett, Durham
TELEPHONE	(043) 475.251
NUMBER OF ROOMS	17 rooms
RATES	Single room with bath from £16 to £18 per person per night. Double rooms with bath and breakfast from £29 to £32 per night. Two nights with breakfasts and dinners from £34 to £37 per person. Low season rates in effect from March 1 to May

23 and from November 1 to
February 28

OPEN   Year-round
OWNER-MANAGER   Ermes F. Oretti

The LYGON ARMS

The Lygon Arms is located in the village of Broadway on the main road between London and Wales via Oxford. The village is over a thousand years old, and Lygon has been a local inn since the time of Henry VIII. Although the first mention of Lygon appears in records dating back to 1532, the inn is believed to be about six hundred years old.

King Charles I was once a guest here and one room, accessed by the original spiral staircase, bears the King's name. In one of the bedrooms, a stone fireplace built into the wall during the fourteenth century still stands. In 1971, the Lygon became the first country hotel in Britain to be honored with the Queen's Award as an outstanding British inn.

ADDRESS   The Lygon Arms
Broadway, Worcestershire

TELEPHONE   (0386) 85.22.55

RATES	Single room with morning tea, bath, and breakfast from £33 per person per night. Double room with bath, tea and breakfast from £30 to £36 per person per night
OWNER-MANAGER	Kirk Ritchie
AGENCY	Prestige Hotels

LYTHE HILL Hotel

A fourteenth-century farmhouse with a restaurant known for its French cuisine, the Lythe Hill sits across from a new hotel with twenty-eight modern rooms and suites. Situated on fourteen acres of woodlands overlooking the Blackdown National Trust Woodlands, it's located about an hour's drive from London.

ADDRESS	Lythe Hill Hotel Haslemere, Surrey
TELEPHONE	Haslemere (0428) 51.31
TELEX	858402
NUMBER OF ROOMS	23 bedrooms with baths, 4 mini-suites, 7 deluxe suites
OPEN	Year-round
OWNER-MANAGER	R. J. Winiecka
AGENCY	Prestige Hotels

The OLD SWAN Hotel

ADDRESS	The Old Swan Hotel Harrogate North Yorkshire HG1 2SR
TELEPHONE	(0423) 504.051
TELEX	57922
NUMBER OF ROOMS	150 bedrooms with bath
OPEN	Year-round
OWNER-MANAGER	Michael Day
AGENCY	Prestige Hotels

PENNYHILL PARK Hotel

ADDRESS	Pennyhill Park Hotel
	Bagshot, Surrey GU19 5ET
TELEPHONE	(0276) 71774
NUMBER OF ROOMS	32 rooms with bath, 2 suites
OPEN	Year-round
OWNER-MANAGER	Ian Hayton
AGENCY	Prestige Hotels

PORTLEDGE Hotel

Portledge is an excellent example of seventeenth-century architecture, standing in sixty acres of private parkland adjoining the Atlantic Ocean. Built around 1234, a thirteenth-century arch of the Chapel still stands. The hotel's dining room is a beautifully plastered ceilinged room with examples of heraldry, and outside, the courtyard is roofed as it was when it was converted into a New Hall in the eighteenth century. The hotel displays fine old furniture, antiques, ancestral portraits, carved stone coats of arms, Spanish armor, and Armada guns. The Spanish Armada courtyard contains timbers from a Spanish galleon.

Owned by the Coffin family since the time of the conquest, Sir Richard Coffin first came to England with William the Conqueror in 1066 and was granted land around Portledge about 1086. A grandson, Reverand John Pine-Coffin, inherited the estate and, by an act of Parliament, in 1797 assumed the name and coat of arms of Coffin.

ADDRESS	Portledge Hotel
	Fairy Cross
	Sideford, North Devon
TELEPHONE	(023 75) 262
NUMBER OF ROOMS	35 rooms, 22 with bath
OWNER-MANAGER	T. J. Pine-Coffin

ROOKERY HALL

Reputedly Georgian in origin and once owned by the Baron von Schroeder, this small English mansion was rebuilt in the middle of the nineteenth century and is acknowledged as one of the finest country homes in Cheshire. Worleston is located two miles from the floral town of Nantwich, with its famous markets and antique shops. The hotel features elegantly furnished rooms and two paneled dining rooms.

ADDRESS	Rookery Hall
	Worleston, near Nantwich
	Cheshire CW5 6DJ
TELEPHONE	Nantwich (0270) 626.866
NUMBER OF ROOMS	6 rooms with bath, 1 suite
OPEN	Year-round except July 20 to
	August 4
OWNER-MANAGER	Harry and Jean Norton
AGENCY	Prestige Hotels

ROTHLEY COURT

Rothley Temple, as the manor house was called for many years, dates back to the thirteenth century, with some mention of a Roman villa on this site as early as 1086. It was granted to the Holy Order of the Knights of Templar by Henry III in 1231, and in 1240 a chapel was built that still stands today. In 1893 the estate was purchased by the Merttens family, who added the south wings and a spacious kitchen. Rothley remained a private residence until 1930, when it was turned into a nursing home. In 1960 it opened as a restaurant hotel. Set on the edge of Charnwood Forest, the Rothley was a favorite stopover point for British royalty during the hunting season.

ADDRESS	Rothley Court
	Westfield Lane
	Rothley, Leicestershire
	LE7 7LG
TELEPHONE	(0533) 374.141
NUMBER OF ROOMS	36 rooms, most with private bath
RATES	Single room from £27 per person per night. Double room from £31 per night. Superior room from £39 per night
OPEN	Year-round
OWNER-MANAGER	Patrick J. Nash

STUDLEY PRIORY Hotel

Dating back to the twelfth century, Studley Priory was a Benedictine nunnery until Henry VIII's dissolution of the monasteries. The estate was purchased by the Croke family and remained in their hands for 335 years. A private chapel was consecrated in 1639 and a north wing added in 1666. With few exceptions, the estate and building appear today as they did during

Queen Elizabeth I's days. The Park family purchased the house in 1961 and converted it into a hotel. Located on thirteen acres of wooded grounds in the village of Horton-cum-Studley, seven miles from the center of Oxford, the priory sits on a ridge with an excellent view of the Blenheim Palace, the Chilterns, and the Vale of Aylesbury.

ADDRESS	Studley Priory Hotel Horton-cum-Studley Oxford OX9 1A2
TELEPHONE	(086) 735.203
TELEX	857777
NUMBER OF ROOMS	19 rooms with bath
RATES	Single room with bath and breakfast from £41.50 per person per night. Double room with bath and breakfast from £31.50 per person per night
OWNER-MANAGER	J. R. Parke

SWYNFORD PADDOCKS

This hotel is an elegant country house, once the home of Lord Byron's half-sister, August Leigh. Located about ten miles from Cambridge, it sits on acreage of a horse farm near Newmarket, the center of England's horse racing and breeding activities.

ADDRESS	Swynford Paddocks Six Mile Bottom Newmarket, Suffolk C98 OUQ
TELEPHONE	(063) 870.234

NUMBER OF ROOMS	20 beds in 12 rooms with bath or shower
RATES	Single room from £30 per person per night. Double room from £47.30 per night
OPEN	Year-round
OWNER-MANAGER	Ian Bryant
AGENCY	Romantik Hotels

THORNBURY Castle

ADDRESS	Thornbury Castle Thornbury Bristol BS12 1HH
TELEPHONE	(0454) 41.26.47
TELEX	44986
NUMBER OF ROOMS	9 single rooms
OPEN	Year-round
OWNER-MANAGER	Kenneth Bell
AGENCY	Relais et Châteaux

TREGENNA Castle Hotel

Tregenna Castle takes its name from a hill on which the castle stands. In 1470, an Irish seaman shipwrecked near Cornwall built the original building—a two-story, granite home with twelve bedrooms. The turrets, along with ten additional bedrooms, were added in 1844. Room number 1 is believed to have been the office of a former Magistrate, Samuel Stephens, a member of Parliament for St. Ives and High Sheriff of Cornwall in 1805. When Stephens died in 1834 the castle was willed to his unmarried son, who sold it in 1888.

When a branch of the railroad opened between St. Ives and St. Erth, the Great Western Railroad leased, then bought, the castle and turned it into a hotel. The first addition, a dining room, was added in 1924. The west wing, with forty-nine bedrooms, began construction in 1929 and was completed in 1932, bringing the total number of bedrooms to ninety.

ADDRESS	Tregenna Castle Hotel P. O. Box 4 St. Ives Cornwall TR26 2DE

TELEPHONE	(073 679) 5254
TELEX	45128
NUMBER OF ROOMS	90 rooms
RATES	Single room with bath and breakfast from £20 to £25 per person per night. Double room with bath from £45 to £55 per night. Low season rates in effect from April 16 to June 14 and September 4 to October 31
OPEN	Year-round
OWNER-MANAGER	N. D. Birrell
AGENCY	BTH

WELCOMBE Hotel

Once owned by Sir George Trevelyan, an eminent Victorian historian, the Welcombe has hosted British royalty and guests like Teddy Roosevelt. Set in 120 acres of woods and parklands, the hotel is the epitome of an English country estate. Bedrooms and suites are available in the modern Garden Wing, as well as the country house. The hotel sits on the banks of the River Avon with a panoramic view of the surrounding countryside. Nearby is Charlotte Park, an Elizabethan mansion where the young Shakespeare was arraigned for poaching in 1585.

ADDRESS	Welcombe Hotel Warwick Road Stratford-Upon-Avon Warwickshire CV37 ONR
TELEPHONE	Stratford 295.252
NUMBER OF ROOMS	154 beds in 84 rooms
RATES	Single rooms with bath and breakfast from £35.50 to £39 per person per night. Double rooms from £90 to £100 per night for two. Special three and seven day rates, including all meals, are available
OPEN	Year-round
OWNER-MANAGER	J. M. Whittingham
AGENCY	BTH

Château de Marçay, *France*

Château du Gué-Péan, *France*

Château du Gué-Péan, *France*

Château du Gué-Péan, *France*

Château de Rochegude
France

Château de Malène, *France*

Château de Malène, *France*

Château de Challes, *France*

Domaine de la Tortinière, *France*

Hôtel de la Cité, *France*

Burghotel auf Schönburg, *Germany*

WEST LODGE PARK Hotel

The West Lodge Park Hotel is a William IV country mansion, completely restored and furnished in elegance. It's located in the rolling countryside just outside of London. It has its own thirty-five-acre park which includes a well-known arboretum with hundreds of rare trees. Centrally located for excursions, it's considered to be one of the finest examples of Jacobean architecture in England. Adjoining the estate is Trent Park, London's country park, a golf course, and riding stables.

ADDRESS	West Lodge Park Hotel
	Hadley Wood
	Barnet, Hertfordshire
	EN4 OPY
TELEPHONE	(01) 440.8311
NUMBER OF ROOMS	54 rooms with bath, 2 suites
OPEN	Year-round
OWNER-MANAGER	Trevor Beal and John Phillip
AGENCY	Prestige Hotels

WOODFORD BRIDGE Hotel

The Woodford Bridge offers thatched-roof country cottages located along the banks of the River Torridge in secluded woodlands near the old market town of Holsworthy.

ADDRESS	Woodford Bridge Hotel
	Holsworthy
	Devon, Milton Damerel
	EX22 7LL
TELEPHONE	(040) 926.481
NUMBER OF ROOMS	22 beds in 7 rooms with bath, 9 rooms with bath or shower
RATES	Single rooms from £11.20 to £24 per person per night. Double rooms from £20.80 to £33 per night.
OPEN	Year-round
OWNER-MANAGER	Mr. Vincent
AGENCY	Romantik Hotels

GREAT BRITAIN: SCOTLAND

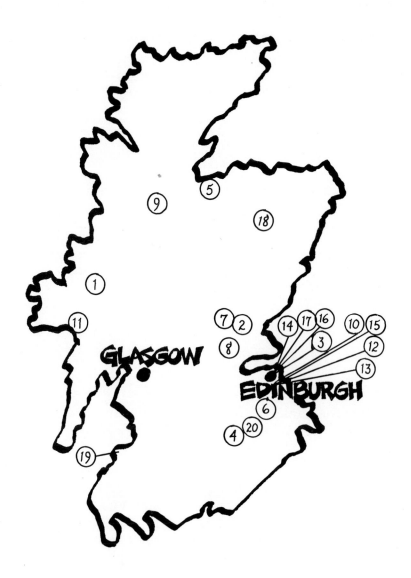

1. Ardsheal House
2. Ballathie House
3. Caledonian Hotel
4. Cringletie House Hotel
5. Culloden House
6. Dalhousie Castle
7. Dunkeld House Hotel
8. Gleneagles Hotel
9. Glengarry Castle Hotel
10. Greywalls

11. Isle of Eriska Hotel
12. Johnstounburn House Hotel
13. Melville Castle Hotel
14. North British Hotel
15. The Open Arms
16. Prestonfield House
17. The Roxburghe Hotel
18. Tullich Lodge
19. Turnberry Hotel
20. Venlaw Castle

CONTENTS

ARDSHEAL HOUSE

Ardsheal sits on a high peninsula, accessible by a private driveway that borders Loch Linnhe. Built of stone and granite, Ardsheal dates back to 1545, when it was built as the manor house of the Stewarts of Appin. During an uprising in 1745 the building was completely destroyed, then rebuilt in 1760. Ardsheal plays an important part in Robert Louis Stevenson's *Kidnapped*, for it was only a mile from the hotel where the infamous murder of Appin took place.

Inside the hotel, you'll find an oak-paneled reception lounge where a fire is usually blazing on the old stone hearth. A second lounge is on the Loch side of the hotel. The dining room faces the garden and has a glassed-in enclosure. Each of the bedrooms is individually decorated.

ADDRESS	Ardsheal House Kentallen of Appin Argyll PA38 4BX
TELEPHONE	(063) 174.227
NUMBER OF ROOMS	12 rooms, 8 with private bath
RATES	Single room with breakfast from £25 to £35 per person per night. Double or twin-bedded rooms from £17.50 to £22 per person per night. Discounts for 4 to 7 night stay when dinners are taken at the hotel
OPEN	Easter to mid-October
OWNER-MANAGER	Jane and Ropert Taylor

BALLATHIE HOUSE

Ballathie sits on two thousand acres in the Parrish of Kinclaven in Perthshire, fourteen miles north of the village. Surrounded by scenic woods and bordered on two sides by the River Tay, the building was built in the French Baronial style in 1880 by General Richard Robertson and purchased by its present owners in 1972.

ADDRESS	Ballathie House
	Kinclaven-by-Stanley
	Perthshire PH1 4QN
TELEPHONE	Meikleour 268
TELEX	727396
NUMBER OF ROOMS	39 rooms
RATES	Single room with breakfast from £22 to £25 per person per night. Double room with bath and breakfast from £42 to £48 per night. Room with two meals daily from £24 to £29 per person per day. Four day stays (Monday through Thursday) including meals from £155 per person
OPEN	Year-round
OWNER-MANAGER	Mrs. P. E. Brassey

CALEDONIAN Hotel

ADDRESS	Caledonian Hotel
	Edinburgh
TELEPHONE	(031) 556.2414
TELEX	72179
NUMBER OF ROOMS	222 rooms

CRINGLETIE HOUSE Hotel

Cringletie is a distinguished mansion set back off the main road between Peebles and Edinburgh in twenty-eight acres of gardens and woodlands. It was formerly the home of the Wolfe Murray family, descendants of Lieutenant Colonel Alexander Murray, who accepted the surrender of Quebec.

ADDRESS	Cringletie House Hotel
	Peebles EH 45 8PL
TELEPHONE	(072) 13.233
NUMBER OF ROOMS	16 rooms, 11 with private bath

RATES	Double or twin-bedded room with bath and breakfast from £17.50 per person per night. Room with breakfast (no bath) from £16.50 per person per night
OWNER-MANAGER	S. L. Maguire

CULLODEN HOUSE

Culloden became famous in Scottish history as the headquarters for Bonnie Prince Charles before the battle of Culloden when the Jacobites were routed by the Duke of Cumberland in 1746. Rebuilt in 1772 in its present form, the hotel is surrounded by spacious grounds and offers two luxurious Princes suites in addition to the traditional bedrooms. Local places of interest include Loch Ness, the battle site of Culloden, and the Moray Mirth.

ADDRESS	Culloden House Inverness, Inverness-Shire
TELEPHONE	(0463) 790.461
TELEX	75402
NUMBER OF ROOMS	21 rooms, all with bath
OPEN	Year-round
OWNER-MANAGER	Kenneth McLennan and James Whyte

DALHOUSIE Castle

Dalhousie dates back to the twelfth century and has played host to Edward I, Henry IV, Oliver Cromwell, and Queen Victoria. Now fully restored to its original style, it's located about eight miles from Edinburgh.

The main section of the current structure was built in 1450 from the red stone quarried from the banks of the River South Esk on which the castle stands. Inside the castle, there's a mural staircase leading down from the banquet hall to the inner dungeons, where prisoners were lowered by rope. Originally, access to the castle was by crossing a drawbridge over a deep, dry moat, but during the castle's conversion into a hotel the moat was excavated and a new drawbridge constructed. the recesses for the drawbridge's counterweights can still be seen above the main door as can the machicolations used by defenders to pour buring oil down on assailants.

ADDRESS	Dalhousie Castle
	Bonnyrigg, Edinburgh
TELEPHONE	(0875) 201.53
TELEX	Dalhous 72380
NUMBER OF ROOMS	24 rooms
RATES	Single rooms with breakfast from £32 per person per night. Double or twin-bedded rooms and suites from £55 per night. Princes Rooms from £45 per night
OPEN	Year-round
OWNER-MANAGER	Anthony Saint Claire

DUNKELD HOUSE Hotel

Located on over one hundred acres of gardens and woodlands along the banks of the River Tay, the Dunkeld house was built in 1900 for the Seventh Duke of Atholl.

ADDRESS	Dunkeld House Hotel
	Dunkeld
	Perthshire PH8 OHX
TELEPHONE	(035) 02.243
TELEX	727396

GLENEAGLES Hotel

Built in 1910, the Gleneagles is a five-star luxury hotel located about forty miles from Edinburgh.

ADDRESS	Gleneagles Hotel
	Auchterarder, Perthshire
TELEPHONE	(07646) 2231
TELEX	76105
NUMBER OF ROOMS	209 rooms

GLENGARRY Castle Hotel

Glengarry is a large mansion-home built between 1866 and 1869 and is located about eight miles from Loch Ness. The castle sits on wooded acreage with an excellent view of Loch Olch. History says the castle was built with stones passed from hand to hand by a chain of craftsmen stretching seven miles from the castle's site to the Ben Tigh. The original building dates back to 1602 but was burned to the ground in 1654. Rebuilt, it was accidentally destroyed by fire in August of 1716. The current building was built around 1727.

ADDRESS	Glengarry Castle Hotel
	Invergarry, Inverness-Shire
TELEPHONE	(080 93) 254
NUMBER OF ROOMS	30 rooms
RATES	Single room without bath from £12 per person per night. Double room with bath from £13 per person per night. Double room with bath, breakfast and dinner from £17.50 per person per day
OPEN	Year-round
OWNER-MANAGER	Mr. and Mrs. MacCallum and Mrs. Peterson

GREYWALLS

A beautiful Edwardian-Lutyens house located on the edge of the Muirfield golf course.

ADDRESS	Greywalls
	Gullane
	East Lothian EH31 ZEG
TELEPHONE	(0620) 842.144
TELEX	727396

ISLE OF ERISKA Hotel

A Scottish Baronial mansion located on a secluded island of the west coast of Scotland, accessible by a private bridge that stretches a full mile across the west coast hills of the Atlantic Ocean.

ADDRESS	Isle of Eriska Hotel
	Ledaig, Connel, Argyll
TELEPHONE	Ledaig 371
TELEX	727396
OWNER-MANAGER	Rovin and Sheena Buchanan-Smith

JOHNSTOUNBURN HOUSE Hotel

Nestled in the Lammermuir hills, about fifteen miles from Edinburgh, the Joynstounburn was built in 1625 and stands behind walled gardens featuring an eighteenth-century gazebo and dovecot.

ADDRESS	Johnstounburn House Hotel
	Humbie, East Lothian
	EH 36 SPL
TELEPHONE	Humbie (087533) 696
TELEX	727897

MELVILLE Castle Hotel

The Melville Castle dates back to the sixteenth century, when it was a hunting lodge used by Mary Queen of Scots. The present building was commissioned by Henry Dundas, the First Viscount of Melville, and completed in 1788. In the library, there are over 2,000 books dating back to the seventeenth and eighteenth centuries, some handwritten by the Viscount. Located on the banks of the North Esk, it's five miles from Edinburgh. A suite with four-poster bed is available, and the castle's dungeon restaurant serves regional dishes.

ADDRESS	Melville Castle Hotel
	Lasswade, Midlothian
TELEPHONE	(031) 663.6633
TELEX	727289
NUMBER OF ROOMS	22 rooms, some with private bath
RATES	Rooms with bath from £30 per person per night, without bath from £27 per person per night. Suite from £35 per night
OPEN	Year-round
OWNER-MANAGER	Mr. M. E. Weibye

NORTH BRITISH Hotel

ADDRESS	North British Hotel
	Princes Street
	Edinburgh EH2 2EQ
TELEPHONE	(031) 556.2414
TELEX	72332
NUMBER OF ROOMS	193 rooms

The OPEN ARMS

This stately manor house is located in beautiful Dirleton village near the Scottish coast and has been a hotel for thirty-three years.

ADDRESS	The Open Arms
	Dirleton, East Lothian
TELEPHONE	(062) 085.241
TELEX	727887

PRESTONFIELD HOUSE

Only two miles from the center of Edinburgh, this seventeenth-century mansion stands on twenty-three acres of private grounds with cattle grazing and wandering peacocks.

ADDRESS	Prestonfield House
	Newington
	Edinburgh, Midlothian
TELEPHONE	(031) 667.8000
TELEX	727396

The ROXBURGHE Hotel

The Roxburghe is centrally located in Scotland's capital city and stands in famous Charlotte Square. Designed in the nineteenth century by Robert Adam, the hotel features elegantly furnished rooms and a dining room known for its international cuisine and regional dishes.

ADDRESS	The Roxburghe Hotel
	Charlotte Square
	Edinburgh EH2 4HG
TELEPHONE	(031) 255.3921
NUMBER OF ROOMS	78 rooms, 61 with bath
OPEN	Year-round
OWNER-MANAGER	Eric Moore and Donald Addison

TULLICH LODGE

ADDRESS	Tullich Lodge
	Ballater
	Aberdeenshire AB5 5SB
TELEPHONE	Ballater 55406
RATES	Room with two meals daily from £30 per person per day

TURNBERRY Hotel

ADDRESS	Turnberry Hotel
	Turnberry, Strathclyde
TELEPHONE	Turnberry (06553) 202
TELEX	777779
NUMBER OF ROOMS	124 rooms
OPEN	Year-round

VENLAW CASTLE

Venlaw was built in 1782 in the Scottish Baronial style of architecture on the site of Smithfield Castle. It sits on six acres of land overlooking the village of Peebles, about twenty-three miles south of Edinburgh.

The earliest reference to Smithfield was during the reign of David II. The castle's name was taken from an adjoining estate, and when the old building was destroyed a new building was built, then extended to its present size in 1854. The Cumming family has owned and operated Venlaw for over thirty years.

ADDRESS	Venlaw Castle
	Peebles EH45 8QC
TELEPHONE	(0721) 20384
RATES	Single room with breakfast from £12.50 per person per night. Single room with breakfast and dinner from £18.50 per person per day. Double room with bath and breakfast from £12 per person per night. Weekly rates, including two meals a day from £115 per person
OWNER-MANAGER	Alastair R. B. Cumming

GREAT BRITAIN: WALES

1. Bodysgallen Hall
2. Ruthin Castle

CONTENTS

BODYSGALLEN HALL

Bodysgallen has played an important role in Welsh history and the lives of its princes since 500 A.D. The oldest part of the present structure is the tower, believed to have been erected during the first part of the thirteenth century as a watchtower for nearby Conwy Castle. Bodysgallen was restored in 1620, and the original castle forms the basic structure of the present building. Currently under conversion are old cottages around the main building.

ADDRESS   Bodysgallen Hall
                   Llandudno
                   Gwynedd LL30 1RS

TELEPHONE	(0492) 831.30
TELEX	8951430
NUMBER OF ROOMS	19 rooms with bath
RATES	Single room with bath and breakfast from £25 to £30 per person per night. Double rooms from £40 to £60 per night
OPEN	Year-round
OWNER-MANAGER	Nicholas Crawley

RUTHIN Castle

Ruthin Castle is an original stone and wood Welsh castle built in the year 1296 by Reginald de Gray, a Justice of Cheshire under Edward I. Its stormy history includes an unsuccessful siege in 1400 and complete destruction following the Civil War of 1642. The de Grays remained at Ruthin until the estate was granted to the illegitimate son of Henry VIII, Henry Fitzroy, the Duke of Richmond. Upon his death it was passed on to Welsh officials, who eventually dismantled what remained of the castle. Rebuilt in 1826, Ruthin was a private home until 1963, when it opened its doors as a hotel. It's located on thirty acres of parkland just outside the village of Ruthin in northern Wales.

ADDRESS	Ruthin Castle Ruthin, Clwyd LL15 2NU
TELEPHONE	Ruthin 2264
TELEX	61169
NUMBER OF ROOMS	64 rooms
RATES	Single room with bath and breakfast from £18 per night per person. Double room with bath and breakfast from £16.50 per person per night. Three-day stays with room and all meals from £24.90 per person per day son per day
OPEN	Year-round
OWNER-MANAGER	A. Warburton

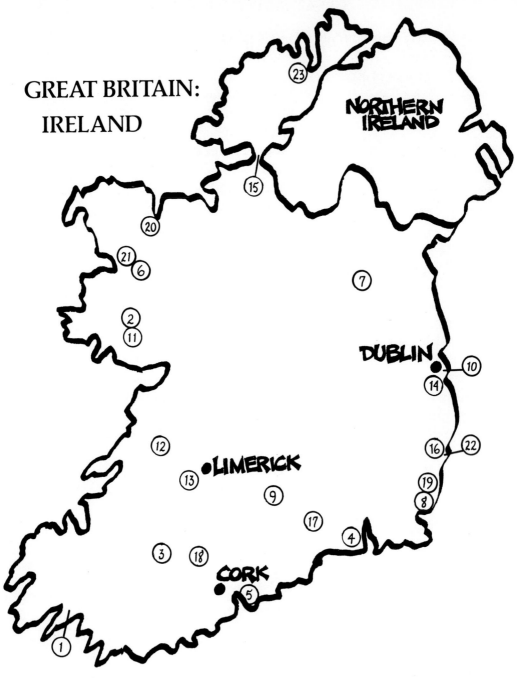

GREAT BRITAIN:
IRELAND

1. Ard Na Greine Inn
2. Ashford Castle
3. Assolas Country House
4. Ballinakill House
5. Ballymaloe House
6. Breaffy House
7. Cabra Castle
8. Cahore Castle
9. Cashel House
10. The Court Hotel
11. Currarevagh House
12. Dromoland Castle
13. Dunraven Arms
14. Fitzpatrick Castle Hotel
15. The Great Northern Hotel
16. The Hunter's Lodge
17. Inishlounaght House
18. Lougueville House
19. Marlfield House
20. Mount Falcon Castle
21. Newport House
22. The Old Rectory
23. Rathmullan House
24. Roseleague Manor

CONTENTS

ARD NA GREINE Inn

Originally an eighteenth-century farmhouse, Ard Na Greine is located one mile west of the fishing village of Schull. Locally caught seafood is featured at the inn's restaurant. The inn is close to some of Ireland's best beaches and Miden Head.

ADDRESS	Ard Na Greine Inn
	Schull, County Cork
TELEPHONE	(028) 281.81
RATES	Single room with bath and
	breakfast from £15 to £17.45
	per person per night
OPEN	Easter to September 30
OWNER-MANAGER	Francis and Rhona Sullivan
AGENCY	Irish Country House and
	Restaurant Assn.

ASHFORD Castle

With a history dating back over five hundred years, Ashford incorporates a thirteenth-century castle and an eighteenth-century French-style chateau on a sprawling estate.

ADDRESS	Ashford Castle
	Cong, County Mayo
TELEPHONE	(094) 226.44
NUMBER OF ROOMS	77 rooms with bath
OPEN	May through December

ASSOLAS COUNTRY HOUSE

The Assolas Country House is a charming, seventeenth-century country home set against a backdrop of sweeping lawns and ancient trees. Within an hour's drive from Killarney and Blarney Castle, the Assolas was the winner of the 1975 National Gardens Award and a runner-up in 1977. All of the rooms are beautifully decorated, and many have wide doors opening up on the estate's gardens.

ADDRESS	Assolas Country House
	Kanturk, County Cork
TELEPHONE	Kanturk 15
RATES	Single rooms with bath and
	breakfast from £12.50 to £15
OPEN	April 30 to October 1
OWNER-MANAGER	Hugh and Eleanore Bourke
AGENCY	Irish Country House and
	Restaurant Assn.

BALLINAKILL HOUSE

Located about two miles from the village of Waterford in rural surroundings within a hundred yards of the River Suir, the Ballinakill offers luxuriously furnished rooms, an eighteenth-century drawing room and a sixteenth-century dining room. All of the dishes served at the Ballinakill's restaurant are prepared with fresh produce and freshly-caught game.

ADDRESS	Ballinakill House
	Waterford
	County Waterford
TELEPHONE	(051) 741.38
RATES	Single room with bath and breakfast from £20 per person per night
OPEN	Year-round except Christmas week
OWNER-MANAGER	George and Susan Gossip
AGENCY	Irish County House and Restaurant Assn.

BALLYMALOE HOUSE

Ballymaloe is a Norman castle hotel, built around 1450 by the illegitimate descendants of the Knights of Kerry.

ADDRESS	Ballymaloe House
	Shanagarrym Midleton
	County Cork
TELEPHONE	(021) 652.531
NUMBER OF ROOMS	25 rooms
RATES	Single room with bath and breakfast from £15.80 to £18.95 per person per night
OPEN	Year-round except Christmas
OWNER-MANAGER	Ivan and Myrtle Allen
AGENCY	Irish Country House and Restaurant Assn.

BREAFFY HOUSE

ADDRESS	Breaffy House
	Castlebar, County Mayo
TELEPHONE	(094) 220.33
TELEX	33790
NUMBER OF ROOMS	41 rooms with baths or showers

RATES   Single room with bath and
               breakfast from £19 per person
               per night. Double rooms with
               bath and breakfast from £13
               per person per night
OPEN   Year-round

CABRA Castle

ADDRESS   Cabra Castle
                   Kingscourt, County Cavan
TELEPHONE   (042) 671.60
NUMBER OF ROOMS   24 rooms with bath or shower
RATES   Single rooms with bath and
                   breakfast from £12 to £14.75
                   per person per night. Double
                   rooms with bath and two meals
                   daily from £16 to £20.50 per
                   person per day, £82 to £125 per
                   person per week
OPEN   Year-round

CAHORE Castle

ADDRESS	Cahore Castle
	Cahore, County Wexford
TELEPHONE	(055) 273.38
NUMBER OF ROOMS	11 rooms
RATES	Single room with bath and breakfast from £8 per person per night. Double room from £7 per person per night. Room with two meals daily from £15 per person per day, £100 per person per week
OPEN	May 1 to September 30

CASHEL HOUSE

Cashel House is an elegant Palladian mansion built in the 1730s, and once served as the residence of the archbishop. Located in the historic village of Cashel, it's surrounded by a walled garden with trees dating back to 1702, planted on the estate to commemorate the coronation of Queen Anne.

ADDRESS	Cashel House
	Cashel, County Tipperary
TELEPHONE	(062) 61.441
TELEX	26938
RATES	Single rooms with bath and breakfast from £15 to £20 per person per night
OPEN	Year-round except Christmas
OWNER-MANAGER	Declan and Patsy Ryan
AGENCY	Irish Country House and Restaurant Assn., Relais et Châteaux

The COURT Hotel

ADDRESS	The Court Hotel
	Killiney, County Dublin
TELEPHONE	(01) 851.622
TELEX	33244
NUMBER OF ROOMS	34 rooms with bath or shower

RATES   Single room with bath and breakfast from £17 to £19.50 per person per night. Double rooms from £15 to £20 per person per night. Room with two meals daily from £28 to £36 per person per day, £171 to £243 per person per week

OPEN   Year-round

CURRAREVAGH HOUSE

Currarevagh House is a mid-nineteenth-century country home located on private woodlands just off the Lough Corrib.

ADDRESS   Currarevagh House
Oughterard, Connemara
County Galaway

TELEPHONE   (091) 823.13

RATES   Single room with bath and breakfast from £15.50 per person per night

OPEN   Easter to early October

OWNER-MANAGER   Harry and June Hodgson

AGENCY   Irish Country House and Restaurant Assn.

DROMOLAND Castle

ADDRESS	Dromoland Castle
	Newmarket-on-Fergus
	County Clare
TELEPHONE	(061) 711.44
TELEX	26854
NUMBER OF ROOMS	67 rooms
RATES	Single room from £56 per person per night
OPEN	March 1 to November 1
OWNER-MANAGER	B. P. McDonough

DUNRAVEN ARMS

ADDRESS	Dunraven Arms
	Adare, County Limerick
TELEPHONE	(061) 94.209
TELEX	70202
NUMBER OF ROOMS	25 rooms with bath

RATES
Single room with bath and breakfast from £15.50 to £18.25 per person per night. Double rooms from £11.95 to £14.75 per night

OPEN
Year-round

FITZPATRICK Castle Hotel

The castle was built by Colonel John Mapes in 1741 and was originally called Mount Napes. In 1770 Henry Loftus, Viscount of Ely, bought the castle and changed its name to Loftus Hill. In 1790 the estate was purchased by Lord Clonmel, who improved the grounds and stocked the estate with deer. The castle is owned by Paddy and Eithne Fitzpatrick, who have strived to provide old-fashioned elegance and personal service.

ADDRESS
Fitzpatrick Castle Hotel
Killiney, County Dublin

TELEPHONE
851333

TELEX
30353

NUMBER OF ROOMS
48 rooms

RATES
Superior single room from £24.80 per person per night (low season) to £37 per night (high season). Victorian Suite from £65 to £88 per night. Castle Suite from £72 to £98 per night

OPEN   Year-round
OWNER-MANAGER   Paddy Fitzpatrick

The GREAT NORTHERN Hotel

ADDRESS   Great Northern Hotel
                    Bundoran, County Donegal
TELEPHONE   (072) 412.04
NUMBER OF ROOMS   96 rooms with bath
OPEN   March through December
OWNER-MANAGER   Anthony and Breege Timony

The HUNTER'S LODGE

The Hunter's Lodge is one of Ireland's oldest coaching inns, now owned by the fifth generation of the original owners. Located along the banks of the River Vartry and surrounded by gardens, the lodge's restaurant features fresh fish from the sea, game, roasts, and vegetables from the estate's gardens.

ADDRESS   The Hunter's Lodge
                    Rathnew, County Wicklow
TELEPHONE   (0404) 4106
NUMBER OF ROOMS   17 rooms, some with bath
RATES   Single rooms with bath and
                    breakfast from £12.50 per per-
                    son per night

OWNER-MANAGER   Mrs. Maureen Gellettie
AGENCY   Irish Country House and
Restaurant Assn.

INISHLOUNAGHT HOUSE

Located in the village of Marlfield at the foot of the Camoeragh Mountains, the Inishlounaght is a beautiful Georgian home surrounded by gardens, terraces, and wooded walks.

ADDRESS   Inishlounaght House
Marlfield, Clonmel
County Tipperary

TELEPHONE   (052) 228.47

RATES   Single room with bath from
£15 per person per night

OPEN   April 1 to November 1

OWNER-MANAGER   Evie and Eve Reilly

AGENCY   Irish Country House and
Restaurant Assn.

LONGUEVILLE HOUSE

Built in 1720, Longueville is a historic Georgian mansion home set on five hundred acres overlooking one of the most beautiful rivers in Ireland, the Blackwater. Located an hour from Killarney in southwestern Ireland, the area is famous for its salmon and trout fishing. The food at the Longueville's restaurant is produced from the estate's farm and gardens and cooked by Jane O'Callaghan, a Cordon-Bleu-trained chef.

ADDRESS	Longueville House
	Mallow, County Cork
TELEPHONE	(022) 271.56
NUMBER OF ROOMS	20 rooms with bath
RATES	Single room with bath and breakfast from £17.50 per person per night. Room with two meals daily from £182 per person per week
OPEN	Easter to mid-October
OWNER-MANAGER	Michael and Jane O'Callaghan
AGENCY	Irish Country House and Restaurant Assn.

MARLFIELD HOUSE

Marlfield is a fine Regency-period home on thirty-five acres, the former residence of the Earl of Courtown. Located on the Gorey-Courtown road, it's about thirty-five miles from Dublin.

ADDRESS	Marlfield House
	Gorey, County Wexford
TELEPHONE	(055) 211.24
RATES	Single room with bath and breakfast from £18.50 to £19.80 per person per night
OPEN	February 14 to September 15
OWNER-MANAGER	Mary Bowe
AGENCY	Irish Country House and Restaurant Assn.

MOUNT FALCON Castle

ADDRESS	Mount Falcon Castle
	Ballina, County Mayo
TELEPHONE	(096) 211.72
TELEX	26396
RATES	Single rooms with bath and breakfast from £20 per person per night. Room with two meals daily from £30.50 per person per day. Room with three meals daily from £35 per person per day
OPEN	Year-round except Christmas week
OWNER-MANAGER	Mrs. C. Aldridge
AGENCY	Irish Country House and Restaurant Assn.

NEWPORT HOUSE

A historic Georgian home in gardens and parks adjoining the village of Newport and overlooking Newport River. This manor house has been in the same family for over two hundred years.

ADDRESS	Newport House
	Newport, County Mayo
TELEPHONE	(098) 412.22
TELEX	33740
RATES	Single room with bath and

	breakfast from £15 to £18 per person per night
OPEN	April through September
OWNER-MANAGER	Francis and Elanor Mumford-Smith
AGENCY	Irish Country House and Restaurant Assn., Relais et Châteaux

The OLD RECTORY

The Old Rectory is a lovingly restored 1870s home with high ceilings, fine plasterwork, and bright bedrooms furnished with period antiques. Set on spacious grounds, it's located on the Dublin side of the quaint harbor town of Wicklow.

ADDRESS	The Old Rectory Wicklow Town County Wicklow
TELEPHONE	(0404) 2048
RATES	Single room with bath and breakfast from £17.50 per person per night
OPEN	June 1 to December 30
OWNER-MANAGER	Paul and Linda Saunders
AGENCY	Irish Country House and Restaurant Assn.

RATHMULLAN HOUSE

Rathmullan sits on the shores of Lough Swilly, surrounded by gardens, sweeping lawns and trees sloping down to the beach. The drawing rooms and library have log and turf fires, and parts of the cellar have been turned into an unusual bar. During the summer, lunch is served in an eighteenth-century kitchen, and dinner is served nightly at the Rathmullan's award-winning Pavillion Restaurant.

ADDRESS	Rathmullan House Rathmullan County Donegal
TELEPHONE	Rathmullan 4

NUMBER OF ROOMS	Hotel rooms and 20 beach chalets that will sleep six people
RATES	Single room with bath and breakfast from £12 to £20 per person per night
OPEN	Easter to early October
OWNER-MANAGER	Bob and Robin Wheeler
AGENCY	Irish Country House and Restaurant Assn., Relais et Châteaux

ROSELEAGUE MANOR

ADDRESS	Roseleague Manor Letterfrack County Galway
TELEPHONE	Moynard 7
RATES	Single room with bath and breakfast from £14 to £18 per person per night
OPEN	Easter to November
OWNER-MANAGER	Patrick and Ann Foyle
AGENCY	Irish Country House and Restaurant Assn.

ITALY

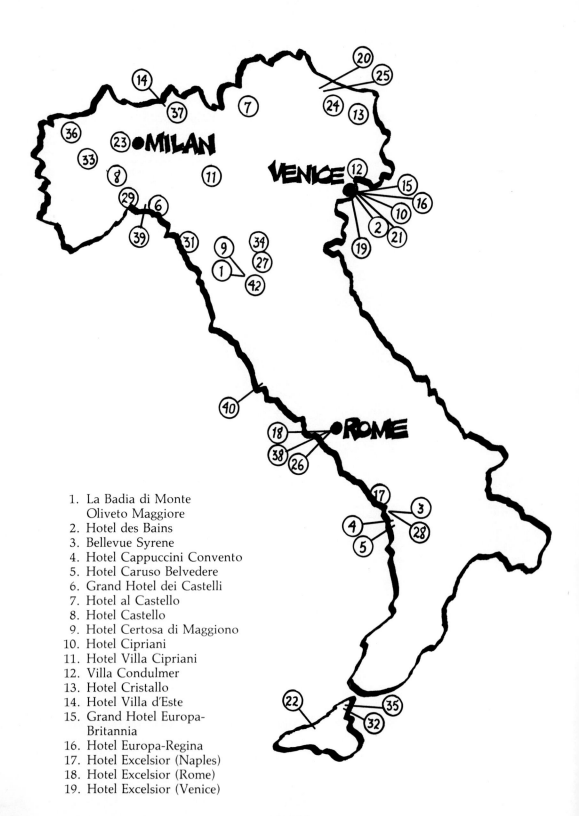

1. La Badia di Monte Oliveto Maggiore
2. Hotel des Bains
3. Bellevue Syrene
4. Hotel Cappuccini Convento
5. Hotel Caruso Belvedere
6. Grand Hotel dei Castelli
7. Hotel al Castello
8. Hotel Castello
9. Hotel Certosa di Maggiono
10. Hotel Cipriani
11. Hotel Villa Cipriani
12. Villa Condulmer
13. Hotel Cristallo
14. Hotel Villa d'Este
15. Grand Hotel Europa-Britannia
16. Hotel Europa-Regina
17. Hotel Excelsior (Naples)
18. Hotel Excelsior (Rome)
19. Hotel Excelsior (Venice)

20. Hotel Castel Freiberg
21. Hotel Palazzo Gritti
22. Grand Hotel Villa Igiea
23. Hotel delle Isole Borromee
24. Castel Schloss Korb
25. Hotel Castel Labers
26. Hotel Lord Byron
27. Villa la Massa
28. Parco dei Principi
29. Park Hotel
30. Il Pellicano
31. Villa la Principessa

32. Hotel Palazzo San Domenico
33. Castello di San Giorgio
34. Villa San Michele
35. Villa San Pancrazio
36. Villa Sassi
37. Villa Serbelloni
38. Sole al Pantheon
39. Albergo Splendido
40. Hotel Torre di Cala Piccola
41. Villa el Toula
42. Villa Villoresi

CONTENTS

La BADIA DI MONTE OLIVETO MAGGIORE

A hotel built around a cluster of buildings dating back to the fourteenth century. The hotel features a Gothic abbey, library, small churches, chapels, and a watchtower.

ADDRESS   La Badia di Monte Oliveto
                           Maggiore

	53020 Asciano, Siena
TELEPHONE	(0577) 707.017
OPEN	Year-round

Hotel des BAINS

The hotel is located directly on Lido beach in a beautiful park setting.

ADDRESS	Hotel des Bains
	Lungomare Marconi 17
	Venice-Lido
TELEPHONE	(041) 765.921
TELEX	410142
NUMBER OF ROOMS	270 rooms, 2 suites
RATES	Single room with bath from
	100,000L per person per night.
	Double rooms from 160,000L
	for two. Suites from 290,000L
	to 360,000L per day. Room
	with two meals daily from
	140,000L per person
OPEN	April to October
AGENCY	Cigahotels

BELLEVUE SYRENE

An eighteenth-century villa hotel.

ADDRESS	Bellevue Syrene
	80067 Sorrento
TELEPHONE	(081) 878.1024
TELEX	71333
NUMBER OF ROOMS	50 rooms
OPEN	Year-round

Hotel CAPPUCCINI CONVENTO

A twelfth-century church and cloister.

ADDRESS	Hotel Cappuccini Convento
	84011 Amalfi (Salerno)
TELEPHONE	(089) 871.008
NUMBER OF ROOMS	48 rooms

Hotel CARUSO BELVEDERE

Located almost a thousand feet above the Mediterranean coast, the Caruso Belvedere dates back to the eleventh century. Ravello was founded by the Normans and features Arabic-Sicilian palaces, an eleventh-century cathedral, and the Palazzo Rufolo which dates back to the eleventh century.

ADDRESS	Hotel Caruso Belvedere
	84010 Ravello (Salerno)
TELEPHONE	(089) 857.111
NUMBER OF ROOMS	6 rooms without bath, 20 rooms with bath
RATES	Single room from 7,000L to 21,000L per person per night. Double rooms from 18,000L per night per person. Three-day stays with room and all meals from 36,000L to 55,000L per

	person. Low season rates in effect from January 1 to April 2, April 19 to May 31, October 1 to December 21
OPEN	Year-round
OWNER-MANAGER	Gino Caruso

Grand Hotel dei CASTELLI

The modern hotel is built around the remains of an old castle, situated in a park with an oustanding ocean view. Lifts are provided to a natural, private beach, and an outdoor terrace restaurant is used during good weather.

ADDRESS	Grand Hotel dei Castelli Via Penisola 26 16039 Sestri Levante (Genoa)
TELEPHONE	(0185) 41.044
NUMBER OF ROOMS	45 rooms

Hotel al CASTELLO

Dating back to the thirteenth century, this castle hotel was formerly the seat of the Pergine Family.

ADDRESS	Hotel al Castello Pergine Valsugana 38057 Trento
TELEPHONE	(0461) 51.158
NUMBER OF ROOMS	23 rooms

Hotel CASTELLO

A fourteenth-century fortress hotel.

ADDRESS	Hotel Castello 15010 Melazzo (Alessandria)
TELEPHONE	(0144) 41.113
NUMBER OF ROOMS	8 rooms

Hotel CERTOSA DI MAGGIANO

ADDRESS	Hotel Certosa di Maggiano
	Via Certosa 82
	53100 Siena
TELEPHONE	(0577) 28.81.80
TELEX	574221
NUMBER OF ROOMS	5 rooms, 9 apartments
RATES	Single room from 150,000L.
	Apartments from 220,000L
OPEN	Year-round except December 16
	to February 28
OWNER-MANAGER	Anna Recordati

Hotel CIPRIANI

ADDRESS	Hotel Cipriani
	Giudecca 10
	30123 Venice
TELEPHONE	(041) 70.7744
TELEX	410062
NUMBER OF ROOMS	77 rooms, 17 apartments
RATES	Single room from 175,000L to
	240,000L. Apartments from
	430,000L to 650,000L
OPEN	Year-round
OWNER-MANAGER	Natale Rusconi
AGENCY	Relais et Châteaux

Hotel Villa CIPRIANI

The former Villa Cipriani dates back to the sixteenth and seventeenth century and is located in the center of the old town of Asolo.

ADDRESS	Hotel Villa Cipriani
	Via Canova 298
	Asolo (Treviso)
TELEPHONE	(423) 55.444
TELEX	411060

NUMBER OF ROOMS	32 rooms with bath, 2 with terraces
RATES	Single room with bath from 87,000L per person per night. Double rooms from 125,000L per night. Room with two meals daily from 95,000L per person
OPEN	Year-round
OWNER-MANAGER	Giuseppe Kamenar
AGENCIES	Cigahotels, Relais et Châteaux

Villa CONDULMER

An eighteenth-century Venetian villa, built on the ruins of an old monastery.

ADDRESS	Villa Condulmer 31020 Mogliano Veneto-Zerman (Treviso)
TELEPHONE	(041) 450.001
NUMBER OF ROOMS	33 rooms

Hotel CRISTALLO

ADDRESS	Hotel Cristallo Via R. Menardi 42 Cortina d'Ampezzo
TELEPHONE	(436) 4281
TELEX	440090
NUMBER OF ROOMS	86 rooms, 9 suites
RATES	Room with three meals daily from 85,000L (low season) to 110,000L (high season). Double room with three meals daily from 75,000L to 100,000L per person per day
OPEN	Year-round
AGENCY	Cigahotels

Hotel Villa d'ESTE

An elegant villa hotel built in 1568.

ADDRESS	Hotel Villa d'Este Via Regina 40 22010 Cernobbia (Como)
TELEPHONE	(031) 51.14.71
TELEX	38025
NUMBER OF ROOMS	154 rooms, 27 apartments
RATES	Single room with breakfast from 173,000L per person per night. Apartments with bath and breakfast from 234,000L to 338,000L per night
OPEN	April to October

Grand Hotel EUROPA-BRITANNIA

A seventeenth-century Venetian palace, formerly a private residence.

ADDRESS	Grand Hotel Europa-Britannia
	San Marco 2159
	30124 Venice
TELEPHONE	(041) 70.04.77
TELEX	41123
NUMBER OF ROOMS	140 rooms
OPEN	Year-round

Hotel EUROPA-REGINA

Overlooking the Grand Canal in Venice, opposite Santa Maria della Salute and near St. Mark's Square, the Hotel Regina features terrace dining and free passenger service between Venice and the Lido.

ADDRESS	Hotel Europa-Regina
	San Marco 2159
	Canal Grande
	30124 Venice
TELEPHONE	(041) 700.477
TELEX	410123
NUMBER OF ROOMS	200 rooms, 6 suites
RATES	Single room with bath from 90,000L per person per night. Double rooms from 145,000L per night for two. Suites from 190,000L per night
OPEN	Year-round
AGENCY	Cigahotels

Hotel EXCELSIOR

Located in the center of Naples' Old Town, the hotel overlooks the harbor of Santa Lucia.

ADDRESS	Hotel Excelsior
	Via Partenope 48
	Naples
TELEPHONE	(081) 417.11
TELEX	710043
NUMBER OF ROOMS	158 rooms, 10 suites
RATES	Single room with bath from 100,000L per person per night. Double rooms from 150,000L per night for two

Hotel EXCELSIOR

The Hotel Excelsior is located on the famous Via Veneto, near the Gardens of Villa Borghese.

ADDRESS	Hotel Excelsior
	Via Vittori Veneto 125
	Rome
TELEPHONE	(06) 47.08

TELEX   610232
NUMBER OF ROOMS   394 rooms, 38 sites
RATES   Single room with bath from
                     140,000L per person per night.
                     Double rooms from 195,000L
                     per night. Suites from 230,000L
                     to 350,000L per night
OPEN   Year-round
AGENCY   Cigahotels

Hotel EXCELSIOR

ADDRESS   Hotel Excelsior
                     Lungomare Marconi 40
                     Venice-Lido
TELEPHONE   (041) 760.201
TELEX   410023
NUMBER OF ROOMS   245 rooms, 17 suites
RATES   Single room with bath from
                     165,000L per person per night.
                     Double room from 230,000L
                     per night. Single room with
                     bath and two meals daily,
                     203,000L per day
AGENCY   Cigahotels

Hotel Castel FREIBERG

ADDRESS   Hotel Castel Freiberg
                     Fragsburg Via Cavour
                     39012 Merano (Bolzano)
TELEPHONE   (0473) 44.196
NUMBER OF ROOMS   27 single rooms, 5 apartments
RATES   Single room with breakfast
                     from 90,000L to 110,000L.
                     Apartments from 115,000L to
                     140,000L
OPEN   April through September
OWNER-MANAGER   A. Jacopino and M. Bortolotti
AGENCY   Relais et Châteaux

Hotel Palazzo GRITTI

Located in the fifteenth century palace that belonged to the Doge Anrea Gritt, the hotel overlooks the Grand Canal and is situated only a few steps from St. Mark's Square.

ADDRESS	Hotel Palazzo Gritti
	Campo S. Maria del Giglio
	2467
	Venice
TELEPHONE	(041) 26.044
TELEX	410125
NUMBER OF ROOMS	92 rooms, 11 suites
RATES	Single room with bath from 172,000L per night per person. Double rooms from 230,000L per night
AGENCY	Cigahotels

Grand Hotel Villa IGIEA

An elegant hotel surrounded by lovely gardens near a private beach.

ADDRESS	Grand Hotel Villa Igiea
	Via Belmonte 43
	90142 Palermo (Sicily)
TELEPHONE	(091) 54.37.44
TELEX	910092
NUMBER OF ROOMS	118 rooms, 6 apartments
RATES	Room with bath from 125,000L per person per night. Apartments from 225,000L per night
OPEN	Year-round
AGENCY	Relais et Châteaux

Hotel delle ISOLE BORROMEE

Located near Lake Maggiore, the hotel overlooks the Borromean Islands and the Alps.

ADDRESS	Hotel delle Isole Borromee
	Coroso Umberto 1
	Stresa (Novara)
TELEPHONE	(323) 30.431
TELEX	200377
NUMBER OF ROOMS	145 rooms, 6 suites
RATES	Single room with bath from 85,000L per person per night. Double rooms from 125,000L per night. Room with bath and two meals daily from 125,000L per day.

Castel KORB

ADDRESS	Castel Korb
	39050 Appiano, Missiano (Bolzano)
TELEPHONE	(0471) 52.199
NUMBER OF ROOMS	57 rooms

Castello LABERS

Located high over the village of Merano, the Castello Labers offers a panoramic view of the Italian countryside.

ADDRESS	Castello Labers
	Via Labers 25
	39012 Merano (Bolzano)
TELEPHONE	(0473) 26.085
NUMBER OF ROOMS	34 rooms

Hotel LORD BYRON

ADDRESS	Hotel Lord Byron
	Via Giuseppe di Notaris 5
	00197 Rome
TELEPHONE	(06) 360.95.41
TELEX	61127
NUMBER OF ROOMS	47 rooms, 8 apartments
RATES	Single room from 110,000L to 115,000L. Apartments from 160,000L to 180,000L
OPEN	Year-round
OWNER-MANAGER	Amedeo Ottaviani
AGENCY	Relais et Châteaux

Villa la MASSA

The villa is located four miles east of Florence along the Arno River and dates back to the fifteenth century, when it was the home and estate of the powerful Giraldi family of Italy. The estate changed hands in 1753 and was purchased by the Pecori family, who lived here until the beginning of the nineteenth century. Restored to its original sixteenth-century style after suffering extensive damage during World War II, the villa was renovated again after the Arno flood of 1966.

The villa consists of three buildings, each built in a different period style and tucked behind retaining walls along the river. Two of the buildings are connected by underground tunnels that date back hundreds of years. One of the two restaurants is located in an underground room that was once a dungeon.

ADDRESS	Villa la Massa
	50010 Candeli
	Bagno a Ripoli (Firenze)
TELEPHONE	(055) 630.051
NUMBER OF ROOMS	44 rooms with bath
RATES	Single room with bath from 55,000L to 70,000L per person per night. Double room with bath from 75,000L to 104,000L per person per night. Room with two meals daily from 81,000L to 99,000L per person per day. Room with all meals from 104,000L to 122,000L per person per day
OPEN	September through July
OWNER-MANAGER	P. Nocentini

PARCO DEI PRINCIPI

A new hotel built around an eighteenth-century villa once owned by a Sicilian prince.

ADDRESS	Parco dei Principi
	80067 Sorrento
TELEPHONE	(081) 878–2102
NUMBER OF ROOMS	200 rooms

PARK Hotel

The Park is a seventeenth-century castle-style villa built around a fifteenth-century estate.

ADDRESS	Park Hotel
	Corso Italia 10
	16145 Genoa
TELEPHONE	(010) 311.040
NUMBER OF ROOMS	19 rooms

Il PELLICANO

ADDRESS	Il Pellicano
	Cala dei Santi
	58018 Porto Erocle
TELEPHONE	(0564) 83.38.01
TELEX	500131
NUMBER OF ROOMS	28 rooms, 3 apartments
RATES	Single room from 100,000L to 181,000L. Apartments from 146,000L to 281,000L
OPEN	Year-round except October 1 to April 8
OWNER-MANAGER	Emili Ennio
AGENCY	Relais et Châteaux

Villa La PRINCIPESSA

ADDRESS	Villa la Principessa
	Massa Pisana
	55050 Lucca
TELEPHONE	(0583) 37.91.36
TELEX	590068
NUMBER OF ROOMS	39 rooms, 5 apartments
RATES	Single room rom 100,000L to 130,000L. Apartments from 140,000L to 160,000L
OPEN	Year-round
OWNER-MANAGER	Giancario Mugnani
AGENCY	Relais et Châteaux

Hotel Palazzo SAN DOMENICO

ADDRESS	Hotel Palazzo San Domenico
	Piazza San Domenico 5
	98083 Taormina (Sicily)
TELEPHONE	(0942) 23.701
TELEX	980013
NUMBER OF ROOMS	120 rooms, 10 apartments
RATES	Single room from 150,000L.
	Apartments from 250,000L
OPEN	Year-round
OWNER-MANAGER	F. Forlano

Castello di SAN GIORGIO

A tenth-century castle with medieval and Renaissance additions.

ADDRESS	Castello de San Giorgio
	15020 San Giorgio,
	Monferrato (Alessandria)
TELEPHONE	(0142) 806.203
NUMBER OF ROOMS	11 rooms

Villa SAN MICHELE

Formerly a fifteenth-century monastery with loggia, parks, and gardens, this hotel is classified as a national monument.

ADDRESS	Villa San Michele
	Via Doccia 4
	50014 Fiesole (Firenze)
TELEPHONE	(055) 59.451
NUMBER OF ROOMS	31 rooms
OPEN	Year-round

Burghotel auf Schönburg, *Germany*

Rothley Court, *England*

The Castle Hotel, *England*

Welcombe Hotel, *England*

Tregenna Castle Hotel, *England*

Ballathie House, *Scotland*

llathie House, *Scotland*

dsheal House, *Scotland*

Turnberry Hotel, *Scotland*

Bodysgallen Hall, *Wales*

Gleneagles Hotel, *Scotland*

rth British Hotel, *Scotland*

edonia Hotel, *Scotland*

Ruthin Castle, *Wales*

Villa SAN PANCRAZIO

This hotel is built on the site of a Roman villa and set in the second largest garden in Taormina. The original cistern has been converted into a guest recreation room.

ADDRESS	Villa San Pancrazio
	Via L. Pirandello 22
	98039 Taormina, Messina
	(Sicily)
TELEPHONE	(0942) 23.252
NUMBER OF ROOMS	17 rooms

Villa SASSI

ADDRESS	Villa Sassi
	Via Traforo del Pino 47
	10132 Torino
TELEPHONE	(011) 90.05.56
NUMBER OF ROOMS	10 rooms, 2 apartments
RATES	Single room from 90,000L.
	Apartments from 150,000L
OPEN	May through March
OWNER-MANAGER	Giulliano Zonta
AGENCY	Relais et Châteaux

Villa SERBELLONI

Located near Lake Como, the Villa Serbelloni is a seventeenth-century palace hotel with a private beach, parks, swimming pool, and an outstanding view of the surrounding countryside.

ADDRESS	Villa Serbelloni
	22012 Bellagio (Como)
TELEPHONE	(031) 950.216
TELEX	38330
NUMBER OF ROOMS	93 rooms

SOLE AL PANTHEON

An early sixteenth-century hotel, one of Rome's historic landmarks.

ADDRESS	Sole al Pantheon
	Via del Pantheon 63
	00186 Rome
TELEPHONE	(06) 67.93.490
TELEX	68222
NUMBER OF ROOMS	29 rooms
OPEN	Year-round

Albergo SPLENDIDO

The former residence of the Marquise Barate.

ADDRESS	Albergo Splendido
	Salita Baratta 13
	16043 Portofino (Genoa)
TELEPHONE	(0815) 691.95
TELEX	331057
NUMBER OF ROOMS	57 rooms, 12 apartments
RATES	Single room from 70,000L to 135,000L. Apartments from 235,000L
OPEN	Year-round
OWNER-MANAGER	M. Pinchetti
AGENCY	Relais et Châteaux

Hotel TORRE DI CALA PICCOLA

The Torre di Cala Piccola was originally built by the Saracens as a lookout tower that gave a sweeping view of the Mediterranean Sea. The tower rises four hundred feet over the water and is surrounded by a stoned terrace that overlooks a private beach and inlet. The apartments and cottages are linked to the main building by flower-decked paths and steps cut into the sheer rocks. Each apartment and cottage has a private entrance and a terrace facing south, offering a spectacular view of the Mediterranean. Sea trips can be arranged through the hotel (which has its own yacht) to

Giglio Island, famous for its wines. The island is ten miles offshore and dates back to the years when Saracen pirates used it as an island fortress and hideaway.

ADDRESS	Hotel Torre di Cala Piccola
	58019 Monte Argentario
	Porto San Stefano (Grosseto)
TELEPHONE	(0564) 825.133
RATES	Single room with bath,
	breakfast and dinner from
	80,000L per person per day.
	Rooms with all meals from
	90,000L per person per day
OPEN	Year-round

Villa el TOULA

ADDRESS	Villa el Toula
	Via Postumia 63
	31050 Ponzano-Veneto
TELEPHONE	(0422) 96.023
TELEX	410005
NUMBER OF ROOMS	8 rooms, 2 apartments
RATES	Single room with bath from
	56,000L to 100,000L. Apart-
	ments from 150,000L to
	195,000L per night
OPEN	Year-round
OWNER-MANAGER	Franca Manera

Villa VILLORESI

A hotel since the mid-1950s, the Villa Villoresi is a twelfth-century villa located in a large park with gardens.

ADDRESS	Villa Villoresi
	Via delle Torri 63
	50019 Sesto Fiorentino
	(Firenze)
TELEPHONE	(055) 4.489.032
NUMBER OF ROOMS	27 rooms

SPAIN

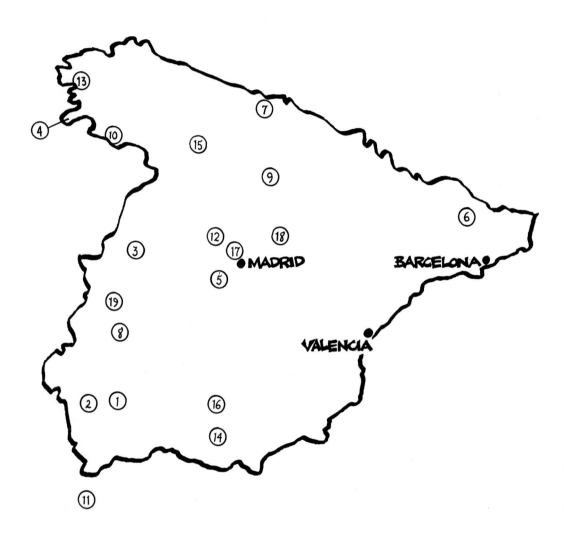

1. Parador Nacional Alcazar
   del Rey Don Pedro
2. Hotel Alfonso XIII
3. Parador Nacional Carlos V
4. Parador Nacional
   Conde de Gondomar
5. Parador Nacional Conde de Orgaz
6. Parador Nacional
   Duques de Cardona
7. Parador Nacional Gil Blas
8. Parador Nacional Hernán Cortés
9. Landa Palace
10. Parador Nacional de Monterrey

11. Hotel la Muralla
12. Parador Nacional
    Raimundo de Borgona
13. Hotel de los Reyes Católicos
14. Parador Nacional San Francisco
15. Hotel San Marços
16. Parador National
    Castillo de Santa Catalina
17. Hotel Santa Maria el Paular
18. Parador Nacional
    Castillo de Siguenza
19. Parador Nacional Via de la Plata

CONTENTS

Parador Nacional ALCAZAR DEL REY DON PEDRO

Built over the remains of the Alcázar de Arriba, one of three Moorish fortresses in the town of Caramona, the Alcázar del Rey Don Pedro was once the residence of King Don Pedro I, the Cruel.

The King turned the estate into a palatial residence that highlighted the Moorish craftsmanship and architecture. The hotel stands on a hillock overlooking the Betis Valley and the village of Carmona. The town is totally surrounded by fortified walls that encircle three Moorish fortress sites, all officially protected as national monuments. Inside the walls, there's a Roman necropolis and amphitheatre, and the town hall displays a complete Roman mosaic. It's located twenty-three miles from Seville.

ADDRESS	Parador Nacional Alcázar del Rey Don Pedro Caramona (Sevilla)
TELEPHONE	(954) 14.10.10
TELEX	PARAL
NUMBER OF ROOMS	102 beds in 8 single and 47 double rooms
OPEN	Year-round

Hotel ALFONSO XIII

Built as a showplace for the Ibero-American Exposition in 1929, the Alfonso XIII is named after the grandfather of the present King of Spain. Set on property within walking distance of the Guadalquivir River and within the shadow of the Cathedral and Giralda, the hotel features arched and colonaded windows, tiled roofs with vaulted towers and minarets, and excellent examples of the Andalucian architectural style.

Inside the hotel, Moorish, Gothic, Italian Renaissance, and Spanish Plateresque art is featured throughout. In the guest rooms, there are closets as large as rooms, black marble bathroom floors, deep, hand-knotted carpets created especially for the hotel by the Royal Tapestry Factory of Madrid, and brocaded couches and overstuffed chairs. Throughout the hotel there are carved cherrywood ceilings, French windows opening onto spacious balconies, and an air of Spanish elegance. Above the door of the Royal Suite on the first floor is the crest of the Golden Crown, and inside are two bedrooms, three baths, a salon, and a kitchen, all decorated with marble tables, seventeenth-century tapestries, and period oils.

Tasseled bell pulls by a cushioned banquet in the gallery outside the hotel's Bar San Fernando silently call your waiter to your table, and at night, maids silently pick up your laundry before you awake and return it early in the day. Less formal, but just as elegant, the

Restaurant Italica has private dining facilities and features many of the regional dishes well known in this area of Spain.

ADDRESS	Hotel Alfonso XIII Seville 4
TELEPHONE	222.850
TELEX	72725
NUMBER OF ROOMS	148 rooms
RATES	Single rooms with bath from 5,200 Psts to 6,000 Psts per person per night. Double room with bath from 8,300 Psts per night. Salon suites from 12,500 Psts to 15,000 Psts per night. Room with three meals daily from 8,000 Psts per person per day
OPEN	Year-round
AGENCY	Entursa

Parador Nacional CARLOS V

The castle, fortress, and monument that make up the Carlos V were built towards the end of the fourteenth century by order of the Condes de Oropesa y Marqueses de Jarandilla. Graceful towers stand at the corners of the grounds, framing a drawbridge and the original fortress walls. The two-storied building centers around a *patio de armas,* adorned with old coats of arms and glazed tiles.

ADDRESS	Parador Nacional Carlos V P.O. Box 15 Jarandilla de la Vera (Cáceres)
TELEPHONE	(927) 56.01.17
TELEX	PARAL
NUMBER OF ROOMS	83 beds in 3 single and 40 double rooms
OPEN	Year-round

Parador Nacional CONDE DE GONDOMAR

The hotel lies within the precinct of Monte Real, surrounded by fortified walls built by the Romans in the second century. In 1474, the castle was captured in battle by Don Pedro de Sotomayor in the name of the King of Portugal, and a private residence was built nearby bearing his name. The L-shaped building of the hotel is a typically Galacian country manor with all rooms overlooking either the Vigo or the Bayona Vias. The clocktower dates back to the sixteenth century, and a watchtower on the grounds is believed to have been in existence in the tenth century.

ADDRESS	Parador Nacional Conde de Gondomar
	Carretera de Bayona
	Bayona (Pontevedra)
TELEPHONE	(986) 35.50.00
TELEX	PARAL
NUMBER OF ROOMS	236 beds in 20 single and 108 double rooms
OPEN	Year-round

Parador Nacional CONDE DE ORGAZ

The Conde de Orgaz, built in a style typical of Toledo, lies between the Sierra de Gredos to the north and the hills of Toledo to the south. Near the River Tagus, the hotel features an excellent restaurant specializing in Castile dishes and rooms furnished in the original style.

ADDRESS	Parador Nactional Conde de Orgaz
	Paseo de los Cigarrales (Toledo)
TELEPHONE	(925) 22.18.50
TELEX	PARAL
NUMBER OF ROOMS	104 beds in 47 double and 10 single rooms
OPEN	Year-round

Parador Nacional DUQUES DE CARDONA

The hotel is a ninth-century fortress spread out around the Church of San Vincente and stands atop a conical hill over the River Cardoner.

ADDRESS	Parador Nacional Duques de Cardona
	Cardona (Barcelona)
TELEPHONE	(938) 69.12.75
TELEX	PARAL
NUMBER OF ROOMS	123 beds in 7 single and 58 double rooms
RATES	Single room from 3,000 Psts per person (low season), 3,500 Psts per person (high season). Double room from 3,500 Psts
OPEN	Year-round

Parador Nacional GIL BLAS

The Gil Blas used to be the country seat of the Barreda-Bracho family and occupies a beautiful manor house with a long history. The house is clearly defined by three architectural periods with an entrance door opening onto a spacious hall with a pebblestone mosaic floor and a well preserved facade of hewn stone. Located in the mountain village of Santillana near the Cantabrian coast, the area has a medieval atmosphere as if the whole village were still in the fourteenth and fifteenth centuries. The Collegiate Church, dating back to the twelfth century, is considered to be one of the loveliest examples of Romanesque art in Spain, and a mile from the hotel, the Cuevas de Altamira, with its caves and prehistoric paintings from the twelfth century, is known as the Sistine Chapel of Primitive Art.

ADDRESS	Parador Nacional Gil Blas
	Plaza Ramón Pelayo 8
	Santillana del Mar
	(Santander)
TELEPHONE	(942) 81.80.00
TELEX	PARAL
NUMBER OF ROOMS	46 beds in 4 single and 18 double rooms
OPEN	Year-round

Parador Nacional HERNAN CORTES

The castle housing the hotel is laid out in a square with round towers at each corner and half towers on the sides. The main entrance to the castle opens onto a patio with galleries supported by Doric and Ionic columns. Built between 1437 and 1443, the hotel's patio is made entirely of white marble.

ADDRESS	Parador Nacional Hernán Cortés
	Plaza de Maria Cristina
	Zafra (Badajoz)
TELEPHONE	(924) 55.02.00
TELEX	PARAL
NUMBER OF ROOMS	50 beds in 28 rooms
OPEN	Year-round0

LANDA Palace

A sixteenth-century castle located less than a mile from the village of Burgos.

ADDRESS	Landa Palace
	Burgos
TELEPHONE	(947) 20.63.43
NUMBER OF ROOMS	39 rooms with bath
RATES	Single room from 4,000 Psts.
	Twin-bedded or double room from 5,900 Psts. Rooms with

three meals daily from 7,500
Psts per person per day
OPEN   Year-round
AGENCY   Relais et Châteaux

Parador Nacional de MONTERREY

The hotel was built in the regional tradition, using cut and
carved stones that give the building an air of elegance. The fortress
of Monterrey faces the hotel, and on the hill where medieval
buildings once stood, it's possible to distinguish the layout of the
primitive, fortified buildings. The area around Monterrey, with its
castles and the Church of Santa Maria de Gracia, is considered to
be one of the most important monuments in the province of
Orense. Pedro I of Castile lived in the castle, and upon his death
the King of Portugal staged an attack on the estate. In 1369, the
castle surrendered to Fernando de Castro, a supporter of the
Portuguese monarch.

The hotel overlooks the Valley of Verin and is located about
300 miles from Madrid.

ADDRESS   Parador Nacional de Monterrey
                   Verin (Orense)
TELEPHONE   (988) 41.00.75
TELEX   PARAL
NUMBER OF ROOMS   45 beds in 1 single and 22 dou-
                   ble rooms
OPEN   Year-round

Hotel la MURALLA

Overlooking the Straits of Gibraltar, this 400-year-old Spanish
fortress is a ranch-style, two-story hotel located between the
copper-domed, seventeenth-century cathedral and the town's
Moorish Tower. Thirty-three of the eighty-three rooms are large,
vaulted-arch suites with vast expanses of terra cotta tile and
Moorish latticed walls. The salon-bedroom units, seventy-three-feet
deep, open onto terraces or balconies facing the hotel's pool. On
the plaza side of the hotel, fifty guest rooms are furnished in white,
pines, saddle leather and deep chocolate brown with picture
window views of the cathedral, the tower, and the sea. Wide lawns
ring Spanish palms and lemon and orange trees, where fashion
shows and banquets are held regularly. Located three minutes by

car from the ferry that crosses the frontier into Morocco, the hotel features two banquet dining rooms.

ADDRESS	Hotel la Muralla
	Plaza Virgen de Africa 15
	Ceuta
TELEPHONE	(51) 49.40
TELEX	78087
NUMBER OF ROOMS	83 rooms with 33 suites
RATES	Single room with bath from 3,600 Psts per person per night. Double room with bath from 5,000 Psts per night. Salon or suite from 6,500 Psts per night. Room with full board from 7,600 Psts per person per day
OPEN	Year-round

Parador Nacional RAIMUNDO DE BORGONA

The Parador Raimundo de Borgona stands on a ridge overlooking the banks of the Adaja River near Castile. Built towards the end of the fifteenth century, it's named after Raimundo de Borgona, a Spanish nobleman who reconquered and reconstructed the city of Avila. The building of the hotel was reconstructed as part of the northern section of the walls in the first quarter of this century, fronting on the square with the Gate of Carmen, one of the nine gates in the wall giving access to the square. The main staircase inside was rebuilt entirely in the old style, using granite and limestone and wrought iron railings. The village of Avila dates back to the twelfth century and was the first fortified Romanesque city in Europe.

ADDRESS	Parador Nacional Raimundo de Borgona
	Marques de Canales y Chozas 16
	Avila
TELEPHONE	(918) 21.13.40
NUMBER OF ROOMS	53 beds in 1 single and 26 double rooms
OPEN	Year-round

Hotel de los REYES CATOLICOS

In the 1400s, the original building that makes up this sixteenth-century hotel included carved wood ceilings, stained glass windows, impressive stone gargoyles, a chapel, and sprawling gardens. It opened in 1503 and was for centuries one of the most important hotels in the Western World. Renovation began in 1953, and two thousand craftsmen worked day and night on the restoration project, without destroying a stone of the original Isabeline facade. All of the sixteenth-century walls, carvings, and cloisters were

restored to their original condition and style. The rooms feature antique writing desks, velvet tasseled cushions, canopied beds, and antique furnishing dating back to the sixteenth century. Within the hotel, Relais, a converted underground stable made of stone, is used for food storage. Suite 330, the Cardinal's Suite with marble bath, fireplace, and a towering red velvet Cardinal's chair, is located next to its own Gothic chapel and can be reserved by request.

ADDRESS   Hotel de los Reyes Católicos
                           Plaza de Espana 1
                           Santiago de Compostela
                           (La Coruna)

TELEPHONE	(981) 58.22.00
TELEX	86004
NUMBER OF ROOMS	159 rooms
RATES	Single room with shower from 3,700 Psts per person per night. Double room with bath from 8,100 Psts per night. Salons and suites from 15,500 Psts per night. Room with bath and full board from 6,300 Psts per night
OPEN	Year-round
AGENCY	Entursa

Parador Nacional SAN FRANCISCO

Situated within the Alhambra precinct, near the fortress and palace of Carlos V, the Parador San Francisco occupies a former Franciscan convent founded by the Catholic monarchs. The convent was built around a mosque and Moorish palace somewhere between 1331 and 1353 by the sixth King of the Nasrid dynasty in Granada, King Yusuf I. The high chapel of the convent was built in the center of the living quarters, and here lay the bodies of Isabella and Fernando until they were moved to the Royal Chapel of the Cathedral of Granada in 1521.

This former Franciscan convent was converted into a hotel in 1944, and in the process of reconditioning the building, a small chapel was built where the church and the sepulchre of the Catholic monks once stood. All of the bedrooms have been kept in a style recalling the eighteenth-century monk's cells, and the galleries are furnished with authentic Spanish furnishings and antiques. The dining room is a showplace for the crafts and skills of Granada's artisans and includes displays of carpets, woven cloth, saddlery, embroideries, mosaics, and iron and copper etchings.

ADDRESS	Parador Nacional San Francisco
	Alhambra (Granada)
TELEPHONE	(958) 22.14.93
TELEX	PARAL
NUMBER OF ROOMS	50 beds in 2 single and 24 double rooms
RATES	Year-round

Hotel SAN MARCOS

High in the plateau regions between Galicia's green mountains and the wheat fields of Castile, the Hotel San Marcos sits on four acres of land behind a facade intricately carved with angel's medallions, cornices, and busts that tell the historic story of this region of Spain. Arranged around a quadrangle of the cloisters and between two formal gardens, all of the guest rooms are furnished in the style of a Renaissance castle, each with an imposing view of the city of León, the surrounding mountains, and the Bernezga River.

The Nuptial Suite sits in a secluded corner of the hotel at the top of a graceful flight of marble stairs and features a covered, four-poster bed sitting on a raised platform separated from the main salon by an ornate, hand-carved railing.

The Royal Suite where King Juan Carlos and Queen Sophia stayed before their coronation is decorated in period antiques and velvets and includes a large living room and reception foyer filled with sculpture, period art, and elegant furniture. Renovated at a cost of almost $10 million, the San Marcos has been a hotel since 1965.

An archaeological museum located in the Sacristy features one of the finest collections of Roman coins, mosaics and stellae, and the world's only Visigothic ivory statue of Christ.

The hotel's lower cloisters are ideal for casual walks through a park filled with pilgrim's shields and statues and Roman headstones dating back to 224 B.C. The upper cloisters, with their rounded columns and arches, overlook a formal fountain and courtyard where meals are served.

Within the hotel, the Abbott once kept his quarters—a four-room complex with rooms opening up onto the church and a balcony overlooking the main altar sixty feet below. Today, weddings are held here.

Within the hotel, there are over a thousand original Spanish paintings, clocks, sculptures, and antique furnishings. The Hotel San Marcos is the site of the International Trout Festival every year, an event that brings six hundred chefs from around the world to prepare their favorite dishes.

ADDRESS	Hotel San Marcos León
TELEPHONE	(987) 23.73.00
TELEX	89809
NUMBER OF ROOMS	258 rooms
RATES	Single rooms from 3,500 Psts to 4,000 Psts. Double room with bath and breakfast from

	5,600 Psts to 6,500 Psts. Suites from 15,000 Psts to 18,500 Psts
Open	Year-round
Agency	Entursa

Parador Nacional Castillo de SANTA CATALINA

The hotel lies on top of the Cerro de Santa Catalina, next to the castle after which it is named. The castle is Moorish in design and sits atop a hill with a commanding view of the Valley of the Guadalquivir and the mountains of the Sierra Morena. From east to south, the buildings of the hotel are protected by inaccessible precipices overlooking a road that leads into the village of Jaén. Within the village, the Cathedral is an excellent example of Renaissance art and was the first church of the diocese to be consecrated.

The hotel's dining room specializes in regional dishes.

Address	Parador Nacional Castillo de Santa Catalina
	Jaén
Telephone	(953) 23.22.87
Telex	PARAL
Number of Rooms	80 beds in 6 single and 37 double rooms
Rates	Year-round

Hotel SANTA MARIA EL PAULAR

This hotel was created from part of a fourteenth-century Benedictine monastery and features a cobblestoned Ave Maria patio, a sixteenth-century chapel, and a restaurant specializing in Castilian dishes from this region of Spain. Rascafría is midway between Madrid and Segovia in an area that offers skiing six months out of the year.

The cloisters, church, and courtyard of the monastery date back to the early 1300s. By 1960 the wear and tear of centuries had the building in disrepair and, having made the decision to align church and state, the black-robed Benedictine monks watched as architects from Entursa began restoring their buildings. The guest rooms were built on two stories around a fourteenth-century patio, and the intricately carved facades, columns, and arches were completely restored in their original style. Red marble, mosaic tiles, and Gothic sculptures are found throughout the hotel, and many of the rooms feature Baroque gilded mirrors, carved wooden cherubs, and monastic portraits.

ADDRESS	Hotel Santa Maria el Paular
	Rascafría (Madrid)
TELEPHONE	(869) 32.00
TELEX	23222
NUMBER OF ROOMS	42 rooms
RATES	Single room with shower from 1,900 Psts to 2,300 Psts per person per day. Double rooms from 3,700 Psts to 4,400 Psts
OPEN	Year-round

Parador Nacional Castillo de SIGUENZA

This historic castle hotel, the seat of almost one hundred Spanish Bishops, is an irregular, four-walled enclosure covering about seven thousand square meters. During the early centuries, the western exit of the castle was used for access into the walls, and subterranean rooms are still accessible. Above the guest rooms is the Dona Blanca, the hotel's elegant restaurant.

ADDRESS	Parador Nacional Castillo de Siguenza
	Siguenza (Guadalajara)
TELEPHONE	(911) 39.01.00
TELEX	PARAL
NUMBER OF ROOMS	161 beds in 3 single and 79 double rooms
OPEN	Year-round

Parador Nacional VIA DE LA PLATA

The Via de la Plata began as a Roman temple, and in 1479 was merged with the Santa Maria Church and converted into a Jesus Convent and Santiago Parish. In 1624 it was used as a hospital and, for a short period during the early 1900s, as a jail. The monks left in 1839, and in 1949 it was opened as a tourist hotel after undergoing extensive renovations. The city of Merida, located on the right bank of the Guadiana River, was founded by Octavian Augustus in the year 25 B.C. as a colony for the veterans of the 10th Legion.

ADDRESS	Parador Nacional Via de la Plata
	Plaza Queipo de Llano 3
	Merida (Badajoz)
TELEPHONE	(924) 30.15.40
TELEX	PARAL
NUMBER OF ROOMS	43 double rooms with bath, 7 single rooms
OPEN	Year-round

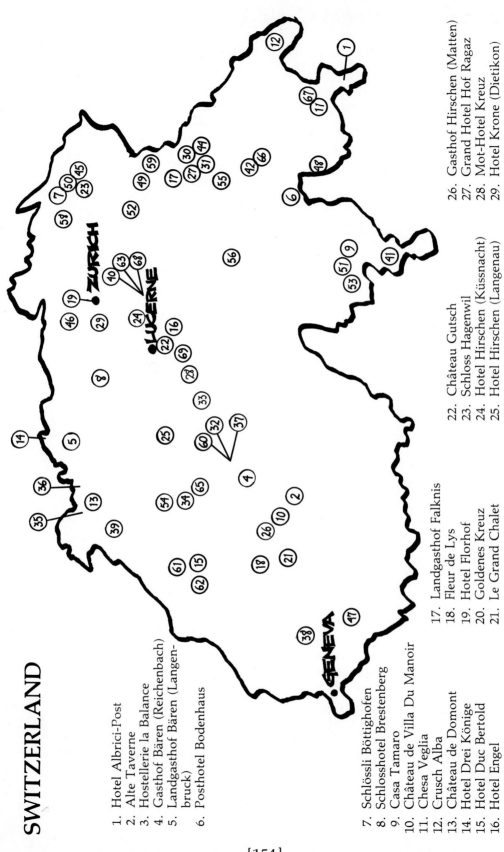

SWITZERLAND

1. Hotel Albrici-Post
2. Alte Taverne
3. Hostellerie la Balance
4. Gasthof Bären (Reichenbach)
5. Landgasthof Bären (Langen-
   bruck)
6. Posthotel Bodenhaus
7. Schlössli Böttighofen
8. Schlosshotel Brestenberg
9. Casa Tamaro
10. Château de Villa Du Manoir
11. Chesa Veglia
12. Crusch Alba
13. Château de Domont
14. Hotel Drei Könige
15. Hotel Duc Bertold
16. Hotel Engel
17. Landgasthof Falknis
18. Fleur de Lys
19. Hotel Florhof
20. Goldenes Kreuz
21. Le Grand Chalet
22. Château Gutsch
23. Schloss Hagenwil
24. Hotel Hirschen (Küssnacht)
25. Hotel Hirschen (Langenau)
26. Gasthof Hirschen (Matten)
27. Grand Hotel Hof Ragaz
28. Mot-Hotel Kreuz
29. Hotel Krone (Dietikon)

30. Hotel Krone (Grusch)
31. Langasthof Krone (Malans)
32. Hotel du Lac
33. Hotel Löwen (Escholzmatt)
34. Gasthof zum Löwen (Worb)
35. Auberge de Lucelle
36. Auberge de Moulin-Neuf
37. Hotel Neuhaus
38. Chateau d' Ouchy
39. Hotel de l' Ours
40. Park Hotel
41. Hotel Patio
42. Post Hotel
43. Alberge della Posta
44. Hotel Schloss Ragaz
45. Zum Römerhof
46. Rote Rose
47. Motel St. Christophe
48. Hotel Palazzo Salis
49. Schlössli Sax
50. Hotel-Restaurant Schloss

51. Schloss-Hotel
52. Hotel Schwert
53. Castello del Sole

54. Hotel Stadthaus Burgdorf
55. Hotel Stern
56. Hotel Stern und Post
57. Hostel Swiss Chalet
58. Hotel zum Trauben
59. Hotel Schlössli Vaduz
60. Grand Hotel Victoria Jungfrau
61. Le Vieux Manoir
62. Relais du Vieux Moulin
63. Seehotel Waldstatterhof
64. Kurhaus Weissbad
65. Gasthof zum Weissen Rössli
66. Weisses Kreuz (Brienz)
67. Weisses Kreuz (Pontresina)
68. Weisses Rössli
69. Hotel Winkelried

CONTENTS

Hotel ALBRICI-POST

This hotel is a fine aristrocratic mansion built in 1682 by the Massella and Bassas families. It has a rich collection of antiques and paintings, and especially notable is the Baroque-style paneling with carved doorways in the Salon des Sybilles. Poschiavo is located on the southern slopes of Bernina Pass near Berne. Excursions to Piz Lagalb, Diavolezz, Val di Campo. Nearby is the Gothic Abbey S. Vittore and the Church of San Carlo in Aino.

ADDRESS	Hotel Albrici-Post
	7741 Poschiavo
TELEPHONE	(082) 501.73
NUMBER OF ROOMS	12 rooms with bath
RATES	Single rooms with breakfast from 30SF per person per night. Single room with three meals daily from 50SF per person per day
OPEN	Year-round

ALTE TAVERNE

A hotel since 1628, the Alte Taverne offers elegantly furnished rooms, a covered swimming pool, artificial ice rink, and tennis court.

ADDRESS	Alte Taverne
	3715 Adelboden
TELEPHONE	(033) 73.17.51
NUMBER OF ROOMS	35 rooms with bath, 22 rooms without bath
OPEN	June 15 to September 30 and December 15 to May 5

Hostellerie la BALANCE

A former horse-changing point dating back to the early nineteenth century, the Balance has been a hotel since it was restored in 1971.

ADDRESS	Hostellerie la Balance
	2332 La Cibourg
TELEPHONE	(039) 22.58.47
NUMBER OF ROOMS	5 rooms with shower
RATES	Single rooms with bath and shower from 33SF per person per night. Single room with shower and three meals daily from 71SF per person per day
OPEN	Year-round

Gasthof BÄREN

This fine old wooden building, built in the style of a Bernese Oberland chalet, was constructed in 1542. All rooms have been furnished in the original country style, and the hotel's kitchen and cellar have earned an excellent reputation in the area for gourmet dining.

ADDRESS	Gasthof Bären
	3713 Reichenbach
TELEPHONE	(03) 76.12.51
NUMBER OF ROOMS	14 rooms without bath
RATES	Single room with breakfast (no bath) from 27SF per night per person. Room with three meals daily from 49SF per person per night
OPEN	Year-round except November

Landgasthof BÄREN

Built in 1577, the first record of this hotel's being renovated dates back to 1746. Now classified as a national monument, the hotel once served as an exchange point for horses used to haul mail coaches over the Swiss Alps. In 1777 the Emperor Joseph II of Austria was a guest, and in 1879 a less welcome guest was Napoleon Bonaparte. The hotel has several dining rooms and an elegant restaurant, staffed by members of the Swiss Guild of Professional Chefs.

ADDRESS	Landgasthof Bären
	4438 Langenbruck
TELEPHONE	(062) 60.14.14
RATES	Single rooms with bath and breakfast from 39SF to 57SF per person per night
OPEN	August 31 to July 1

Posthotel BODENHAUS

The Bodenhaus was built in 1722 by Vicari Johann Paul Zoya after a fire burned down most of the village of Splügen. For over a century, the hotel served as a commercial exchange house for the international movement of merchandise shipped across the Splugen Pass. When a new road was built in 1822, the estate was converted into a hotel. After making the difficult trek over the pass, guests like Queen Victoria, Lord and Lady Hamilton, Prince Louis Napoleon, and Alexei Tolstoy looked forward to their stay at Bodenhaus. The building is a massive cubic building with three stories covered by a sloping roof. The hotel has a number of dining rooms.

ADDRESS	Posthotel Bodenhaus
	7431 Splügen
TELEPHONE	(081) 62.11.21
NUMBER OF ROOMS	25 rooms with bath, 12 rooms without bath
RATES	Single rooms with breakfast (no bath) from 25SF to 30SF. Single rooms with bath and breakfast from 50SF to 60SF. Room with three meals daily from 80SF to 90SF per person per day
OPEN	December 10 to November 1

Schlössli BÖTTIGHOFEN

The castle was built in 1674–76 as the summer residence of the Bishops of Konstanz. Renovated in 1936, it's located on the shores of Lake Constance on its own parkland.

ADDRESS	Schlössli Böttighofen
	8598 Böttighofen
TELEPHONE	(072) 8.20.48
NUMBER OF ROOMS	7 rooms without bath
RATES	Single rooms from 28SF per person per night
OPEN	Year-round

Schlosshotel BRESTENBERG

Located in a park adjoining the Hallwilersee, a nature reservation area, the Schloss Brestenberg was built by Hans Rudolf von Hallwil in 1625. A health resort during the nineteenth century, it opened as a hotel in 1954. All of the rooms are elegantly furnished in period antiques.

ADDRESS	Schlosshotel Brestenberg
	5704 Seengen
TELEPHONE	(064) 54.11.31
NUMBER OF ROOMS	5 rooms with bath, 21 rooms without bath
RATES	Single rooms with breakfast (no bath) from 25SF to 35SF per person per night. Single room with bath and breakfast from 45SF to 60SF per person per night. Room with three meals daily from 55SF to 90SF per night
OPEN	Year-round

CASA TAMARO

Once the finest Patrician house on the Piazza, the Casa Tamaro has been converted into an elegant hotel with artistic and stylistic flair. Built in the late Renaissance style with vaulted ceilings and a picturesque courtyard, the hotel offers boat trips on Lake Maggiore.

ADDRESS	Casa Tamaro
	6612 Ascona
TELEPHONE	(093) 35.39.39
NUMBER OF ROOMS	70 beds
RATES	Year-round

CHATEAU DE VILLA DU MANOIR

Dating back to the sixteenth century, the chateau features the Rainer Maria Rilke Museum on the upper floors and a ground-floor dining room decorated in the original style of the Cantons of Valais.

ADDRESS	Chateau de Villa du Manoir
	3960 Sierre
TELEPHONE	(027) 5.18.96
OPEN	Year-round

CHESA VEGLIA

The Chesa Veglia is a farmhouse, built in the Engadine tradition in 1658. Remodeled as a rustic inn in 1935 by Hans Badrutt, the hotel features the original architecture and is furnished throughout with antiques, artifacts, and frescoes.

ADDRESS	Chesa Veglia
	7500 St. Moritz
TELEPHONE	(082) 3.35.96
NUMBER OF ROOMS	350 beds
OPEN	Year-round

CRUSCH ALBA

The oldest guest house in the Münster Valley, the Crusch Alba was built around 1600 and has been owned by the same family since 1650. The hotel has the look of a private museum and features a unique, old-style Grison dining room.

ADDRESS	Crusch Alba
	7531 Sta. Maria
TELEPHONE	(082) 8.51.06
NUMBER OF ROOMS	2 rooms without bath, 2 rooms with bath
RATES	Single room with breakfast and bath from 35SF to 39SF. Single room with no bath and two meals daily from 41SF per person per day
OPEN	December 16 to October 30

Château de DOMONT

Built in the mid-sixteenth century by the Knights of Vorburg, the Château de Domont was turned into a fortress and Knight's Hall by Jean Conrad de Vorburg and transferred in 1600 to the town of Delémont. Surrounded by woods and meadows, it's furnished and decorated in the original style.

ADDRESS	Château de Domont
	2800 Delémont
TELEPHONE	(066) 22.14.14
OPEN	Year-round

Castles ... [12/13 Paladium 3000] ... Galley 133
manuscript pg. 308

Hotel DREI KÖNIGE

The Drei Könige is the oldest inn in Switzerland, first opened in the year 1026 and for centuries one of the most famous hotels in Europe. Originally called *die Blume* (the Flower), it was renamed Three Kings after the Emperor Conrad II and his son, the future Henry III, met the last King of Burgundy here. Former guests include Napoleon Bonaparte, Voltaire, Charles Dickens, and the Kings of Italy, Sweden, Norway, Bulgaria, Romania, and Spain. Rebuilt on several occasions, the hotel still retains its old-world charm and comfort.

ADDRESS	Hotel Drei Könige
	4001 Basel
TELEPHONE	(061) 25.52.52
NUMBER OF ROOMS	82 rooms with bath, 2 rooms without bath

RATES	Single rooms with bath and breakfast from 90SF to 140SF per person per night
OPEN	Year-round

Hotel DUC BERTOLD

The Duc Bertold is a nineteenth-century nobleman's mansion, renovated in 1969 and since then designated as a national monument. The hotel is named after the Duke Bertold of Zahringen, founder of the village of Fribourg in 1157.

ADDRESS	Hotel Duc Bertold Rue des Bouchers 112 1700 Fribourg
TELEPHONE	(037) 23.47.33
NUMBER OF ROOMS	40 rooms with bath or shower
RATES	Single room with breakfast (no bath) from 39SF per person per night. Room with bath and breakfast from 54SF to 77SF per person per night. Room with bath and three meals daily from 69SF to 107SF per person per day
OPEN	Year-round

Hotel ENGEL

The Engel is considered to be one of the finest and most historic inns in Switzerland. Built in 1405 and enlarged in 1552, the hotel was used by delegates of the Swiss Confederation as a meeting place from 1424 to 1712.

ADDRESS	Hotel Engel 6403 Küssnacht am Rigi
TELEPHONE	(041) 81.10.57
NUMBER OF ROOMS	8 rooms without bath, 2 rooms with bath
RATES	Single rooms with bath and breakfast from 26SF to 60SF per person per night
OPEN	Year-round

Landgasthof FALKNIS

The Falknis has been the trading center of the famous Swiss horse dealer, Andreas Zindel-Badrutt, since 1894. It is now a riding school and horse-training academy, offering guests jaunts on horse-drawn carts to nearby Grison vineyards.

ADDRESS	Landgasthof Falknis
	7304 Maienfeld
TELEPHONE	(085) 9.18.18
NUMBER OF ROOMS	20 beds
RATES	Single rooms with breakfast from 29SF to 32SF per person per night. Room with three meals daily from 52SF to 55SF per day per person
OPEN	Year-round
OWNER-MANAGER	Hans Zindel

FLEUR DE LYS

This rustic-style hotel, built in 1653, stands in the middle of the medieval town of Gruyères and features a gourmet restaurant specializing in regional dishes.

ADDRESS	Fleur de Lys
	1663 Gruyères
TELEPHONE	(029) 6.21.08
NUMBER OF ROOMS	6 rooms without bath
RATES	Rooms with breakfast (no bath) from 35SF per person per night
OPEN	March 1 to February 1

Hotel FLORHOF

A Partrician house built in the mid-1800s, the Florhof was completely restored in 1973–74. Located in a quiet corner in the center of town near the university, it has rooms with stucco ceilings and a pleasant restaurant with an old turret stove.

ADDRESS	Hotel Florhof
	8001 Zürich
TELEPHONE	(01) 47.44.70

NUMBER OF ROOMS	33 rooms with bath
RATES	Single rooms with bath and breakfast from 65SF to 90SF per person per night
OPEN	Year-round

GOLDENES KREUZ

This hotel, rebuilt in the old Bernese style after a fire, offers a fantastic panoramic view of the Alps from room terraces. Stylishly furnished with period pieces dating back to the eighteenth century, it features a grand staircase with late Gothic reliefs, bronze lanterns from Versailles, and a Jägerstüble ball room with a Louis XVI decor.

ADDRESS	Goldenes Kreuz Dorfstrasse 3115 Gerzensee
TELEPHONE	(031) 92.88.36
NUMBER OF ROOMS	9 rooms with bath, 4 rooms without bath
RATES	Single room with breakfast (no bath) from 35SF to 40SF per person per night. Room with bath and breakfast from 45SF to 50SF per night
OPEN	Year-round

Le GRAND CHALET

The largest chalet in Switzerland, built in 1754, the Grand Chalet features carved facades with flower, animal, and coat of arms paintings. A hotel since 1850, its former guests include Victor Hugo.

ADDRESS	Le Grand Chalet 1836 Rossinière
TELEPHONE	(029) 4.65.44
NUMBER OF ROOMS	2 rooms with bath, 30 rooms with bath
OPEN	Mid-December to September except one month in Spring

Chateau GUTSCH

Built on the remains of a thirteenth-century fortress, the Gutsch has dominated the town of Lucerne for over 150 years. It features an old castle cellar and once played host to Queen Victoria of England.

ADDRESS	Château Gutsch
	Kanonenstrasse
	6003 Lucerne
TELEPHONE	(041) 23.38.83
NUMBER OF ROOMS	40 rooms with bath
RATES	Single rooms with bath and breakfast from 73SF to 85SF per person per night. Single rooms with bath and three meals daily from 105SF to 117SF per person per day
OPEN	Year-round except January 3 and February 5

Schloss HAGENWIL

The Hagenwil is a picturesque moated castle dating back to the year 1220. Early in the thirteenth century it was owned by the Knight Rudolf von Hagenwil, a liegeman of the St. Gallen Monastery. It was first restored in 1403. Since 1806 it's been in the hands of the Angehrn family, who still operate the hotel's restaurant.

ADDRESS	Schloss Hagenwil
	8580 Hagenwil
TELEPHONE	(071) 67.19.13
NUMBER OF ROOMS	3 rooms
RATES	Double rooms from 55SF to 60SF per night
OPEN	Year-round
OWNER-MANAGER	The Angehrn Family

Hotel HIRSCHEN

This old wooden house with its large gabled room, built in the style of the Canton of Schwyz, was built in 1640 and has been owned by the same family for over three hundred years. The facade of the house is decorated with twenty-three paintings depicting scenes from the Legend of William Tell. Rooms are furnished in the old peasant style and the hotel's restaurant, the Bauernstube, specializes in regional dishes. Adjoining the hotel is a new building with modern rooms and a cafe-tea room.

ADDRESS	Hotel Hirschen
	6403 Küssnacht am Rigi
TELEPHONE	(041) 81.10.27
NUMBER OF ROOMS	40 beds with bath, 10 beds without bath
RATES	Single rooms with breakfast (no bath) from 28SF per person per night. Single rooms with bath and two meals daily from 56SF to 65SF per person per day
OPEN	Year-round except Christmas

Hotel HIRSCHEN

This inn was first mentioned in a Bernese chronicle as a wine tavern that existed in 1467. The hotel's wine cellar, dating back to the fifteenth century, has a selection of over 28,000 bottles, and can be visited upon request.

ADDRESS	Hotel Hirschen
	Dorfstrasse
	3550 Langnau im Emmental
TELEPHONE	(035) 2.15.15
NUMBER OF ROOMS	6 rooms with bath, 16 rooms without bath
RATES	Single room with breakfast (no bath) from 26SF to 29SF per person per night. Room with bath and breakfast from 35SF to 28SF per person per night. Room with bath and three meals daily from 57SF to 60SF per person per day
OPEN	Year-round except June and January 1–15

Gasthof HIRSCHEN

This Bernese farmhouse, built in the year 1666, has been owned by the Sterchi family for three hundred years. The building was restored in 1960 and has an excellent restaurant specializing in gourmet and regional dishes.

ADDRESS	Gasthof Hirschen
	3800 Matten-Interlaken
TELEPHONE	(036) 22.15.45
NUMBER OF ROOMS	25 rooms without bath
RATES	Single room with breakfast (no bath) from 33SF to 42SF per person per night
OPEN	December 1 to October 25
OWNER-MANAGER	The Sterchi Family

Grand Hotel HOF RAGAZ

This Baroque building, dating back to the seventeenth century, is classified as a national monument and was originally the seat of the Prince-Abbot of Pfafers. Travelers on their way up to the Rhatian Mountain regions used this hotel as a stopover point after it was converted into a hotel in 1846. When mineral springs were discovered there in 1840, the hotel became a popular health resort and now offers a therapeutic and medical department. The hotel features terraces, a grillroom, and private chapel.

ADDRESS	Grand Hotel Hof Ragaz
	7310 Bad Ragaz
TELEPHONE	(085) 9.15.03
NUMBER OF ROOMS	110 rooms without bath, 10 rooms with bath
RATES	Single rooms with bath and two meals daily from 100SF to 140SF per person per day. Bathless rooms with two meals daily from 80SF to 125SF per person per day
OPEN	Year-round

Mot-Hotel KREUZ

The Kreuz consists of four buildings dating back to the eighteenth century. Guests can choose between the elegantly furnished hotel and modern bungalows with covered terraces. The restaurant features an original vaulted ceiling and is furnished with art curios.

ADDRESS	Mot-Hotel Kreuz
	6072 Sachsen
TELEPHONE	(041) 66.14.66
NUMBER OF ROOMS	30 rooms with bath, 30 rooms without bath
RATES	Single rooms with bath and breakfast from 50SF to 65SF per person per night. Rooms with three meals daily from 66SF to 81SF per person per day
OPEN	March to November

Hotel KRONE

Located between Zurich and Baden, the Krone is one of the oldest taverns in the area. Once owned by the Monastery of Wettingen, the current owners' ancestors purchased the building in 1873. It's located in the Limmat Valley.

ADDRESS	Hotel Krone
	8953 Dietikon
TELEPHONE	(017) 40.60.11
NUMBER OF ROOMS	20 rooms with bath or shower
RATES	Single room from 45SF to 58SF per person per night. Double room from 70SF to 92SF per night
OWNER-MANAGER	The Gstrein Family
AGENCY	Romantik Hotels

Hotel KRONE

The hotel was built in the year 1676 and offers beautifully decorated rooms with paneled ceilings.

ADDRESS	Hotel Krone
	7214 Grusch
TELEPHONE	(081) 52.11.16
NUMBER OF ROOMS	50 beds
RATES	Single rooms from 28SF per person per night
OPEN	Year-round except three weeks in Spring-Autumn

Landgasthof KRONE

While the original construction date of the Krone is unknown, in the seventeenth century the estate was owned by Rudolph von Salis. It was rebuilt after the village was destroyed by fire in the late 1700s, then extended to its present size and form in 1802. Owned by the same family for over 150 years, the rooms are furnished attractively, and the hotel's restaurant serves dishes of the region.

ADDRESS	Landgasthof Krone
	7208 Malans
TELEPHONE	(081) 51.14.55
NUMBER OF ROOMS	2 rooms with showers, 4 rooms without
RATES	Single room with breakfast from 30SF to 33SF per person per night
OPEN	Year-round except Christmas

Hotel du LAC

When the first steamboat service began on Lake Brienz, the Hotel du Lac was built and it's remained in the same family since 1888.

ADDRESS	Hotel du Lac Hoheweg 225 3800 Interlaken
TELEPHONE	(036) 22.29.22
NUMBER OF ROOMS	30 rooms with bath, 20 rooms without bath
RATES	Single room with breakfast (no bath) from 39SF to 56SF per person per night. Single room with bath and breakfast from 59SF to 88SF per person per night. Room with bath and three meals daily from 87SF to 123SF per person per day
OPEN	Year-round

Hotel LÖWEN

The Löwen was built in the old architectural style traditional to the Canton of Berne, and is first mentioned in records dating back as far as 1571. At one time, the High Court of Lucerne met in a room on the first floor of the hotel.

ADDRESS	Hotel Löwen 6182 Escholzmatt
TELEPHONE	(041) 77.12.06
NUMBER OF ROOMS	17 rooms
RATES	Single room with breakfast (no bath) from 19SF to 27SF per person per night. Single room with three meals daily (no bath) from 35SF to 70SF per person per day
OPEN	Year-round

Gasthof zum LÖWEN

A former mansion, dating back over six hundred years, the Gasthof zum Löwen was used as a tavern until 1610 when it was purchased by the ancestors of the current owners. In the early fourteenth century, the hotel's Gerichtsstube (court room) was used as a court for the collection of tithes at harvest time. The hotel has a number of salons and private rooms with the original vaulted ceilings and has played host to Professor Messerschmitt and Charles Duke, the Apollo 16 astronaut.

ADDRESS	Gasthof zum Löwen
	3076 Worb
TELEPHONE	(031) 83.23.02
NUMBER OF ROOMS	2 rooms with bath or shower, 4 rooms without bath
RATES	Single room with breakfast (no bath) from 25SF to 30SF per person per night. Room with bath and breakfast from 45SF to 50SF per night
OPEN	July 1 to June 1

Auberge de LUCELLE

Located near the former Abbey of Lucelle on a picturesque lake, this hotel was built in 1690.

ADDRESS	Auberge de Lucelle
	2801 Lucelle
TELEPHONE	(066) 72.24.52
NUMBER OF ROOMS	20 rooms with bath
OPEN	Year-round

Auberge de MOULIN-NEUF

This inn was built in 1692 and was originally a mill, then a sawmill. The building was owned by the Monks of Lowenburg.

ADDRESS	Auberge de Moulin-Neuf
	2801 Roggenburg
TELEPHONE	(066) 31.13.50
NUMBER OF ROOMS	5 rooms with shower
OPEN	Year-round

Hotel NEUHAUS

Formally a transportation point for travelers making trips to the upper end of Lake Thun and the Alpine Passes, the Neuhaus features balconies overlooking the lake and an excellent dining room furnished in the old style.

ADDRESS	Hotel Neuhaus
	3800 Interlaken
TELEPHONE	(036) 22.82.82
NUMBER OF ROOMS	40 rooms with bath or shower,
	40 rooms without bath
RATES	Single rooms with bath and
	breakfast from 46SF to 72SF
	per person per night. Room
	with bath and three meals daily
	from 71SF to 97SF per person
	per day
OPEN	Year-round

Château d'OUCHY

The d'Ouchy is a historic Swiss castle with a tower and Knight's Hall dating back to the twelfth century. Originally the seat of the Bishops of Lausanne, the rooms are furnished in Louis XIII style. Located on Lake Geneva, only five minutes from the mail line railway station and center of Lausanne, it features covered terraces, gardens, and boat excursions.

ADDRESS	Château d'Ouchy
	Place du Port
	1006 Ouchy, Lausanne
TELEPHONE	(021) 26.74.51
NUMBER OF ROOMS	34 rooms with bath, 6 rooms
	without bath
RATES	Single room with bath and
	breakfast from 80SF to 120SF
	per person per night
OPEN	Year-round

Hotel de l'OURS

Located in the wooded pasturelands of the High Jura Mountains, near the ancient Bellelay Abbey, the l'Ours once belonged to a monastery and has been a hotel for several hundred years.

ADDRESS	Hotel de l'Ours
	2713 Bellelay

TELEPHONE	(032) 91.91.04
NUMBER OF ROOMS	4 rooms with shower, 4 rooms without
RATES	Single room with breakfast (no shower) from 24SF per person per night. Room with shower and breakfast from 27SF per person per night
OPEN	Year-round except November

PARK Hotel

Built over the remains of the Löwenstein Castle of the Zumbrunnen dynasty, this hotel sits in the center of a large park with facilities for medical baths.

ADDRESS	Park Hotel 6440 Brunnen
TELEPHONE	(043) 31.16.81
NUMBER OF ROOMS	100 rooms
RATES	Single rooms with bath and breakfast from 49SF to 69SF per person per night. Single rooms with bath and two meals daily from 79SF to 99 SF per person per night
OPEN	March through January

Hotel PATIO

The Patio was built in 1552 and was used as a courtroom, municipal hall, and prison before becoming a hotel. The hotel's courtyard features a fountain that has been declared a national monument, and the hotel's restaurant is known for its Italian dishes.

ADDRESS	Hotel Patio Via Motta 7A 6900 Lugano
TELEPHONE	(091) 2.30.32
NUMBER OF ROOMS	24 rooms with bath or shower

RATES	Single room with bath and breakfast from 45SF to 55SF per person per night. Room with bath and three meals daily from 75SF to 85SF per person per day
OPEN	Year-round

POST Hotel

The Post Hotel is a patrician manor house dating back to the sixteenth century. The former residence of the Barons of Buol, it features inlaid wood paneling and ceilings, family arms carved in wood, arcaded passages, and oil paintings of ancestral figures.

ADDRESS	Post Hotel 7075 Churwalden
TELEPHONE	(081) 35.11.09
NUMBER OF ROOMS	20 rooms without bath
RATES	Single rooms with breakfast from 25SF to 45SF per person per night. Double rooms with three meals daily from 59SF to 69SF per person per day
OPEN	Year-round

Alberge della POSTA

This old mansion hotel dates back to 1767 and was completely renovated and enlarged before opening as a modern hotel. It features an elegant courtyard and Ticenese Room with fireplace.

ADDRESS	Alberge della Posta 6981 Astano
TELEPHONE	(091) 73.18.82
NUMBER OF ROOMS	3 rooms with bath, 17 rooms without bath
RATES	Single room with breakfast (no bath) from 27SF to 38SF per person per night. Single room with bath and breakfast from 38SF to 49SF per person per

Ruthin Castle, *Wales*

Hotel Excelsior (Rome), *Italy*
Hotel Cristallo, *Italy*

Hotel Excelsior (Naples), *Italy*

Hotel Excelsior (Venice), *Italy*

Hotel delle Isole Barromee, *Italy*

Hotel Europe-Regina, *Italy*

tel Palazzo Gritti, *Italy*

Hotel de los Reyes Católicos, *Spain*
Hotel Alfonso XIII, *Spain*

Hotel San Marcos, *Spain*

Hotel San Marcos, *Spain*
Hotel de los Reyes Católicos, *Spain*

Château Gutsch, *Switzerland* (over)
Hotel du Lac, *Switzerland*

night. Room with bath and two
meals daily from 93SF to 104SF
per day

OPEN   March 15 to December 1

Hotel Schloss RAGAZ

ADDRESS   Hotel Schloss Ragaz
                    7310 Bad Ragaz
TELEPHONE   (085) 9.23.55
NUMBER OF ROOMS   48 rooms with bath or shower,
                    14 rooms without bath
RATES   Single rooms without bath and
                    two meals daily from 46SF to
                    73SF per person per day. Room
                    with bath and two meals daily
                    from 55SF to 89SF per person
                    per day
OPEN   February 1 to January 7

Zum RÖMERHOF

The Römerhof inn stands on the corner of the old town wall of
Arbon. Built in 1500, it was a Protestant school from 1784 to 1872.
The half-timbered structure was renovated in 1934 and again in
1968.

ADDRESS   Zum Römerhof
                    9320 Arbon
TELEPHONE   (071) 46.16.08
OPEN   Year-round except June

ROTE ROSE

This magnificent half-timbered building was built in 1245 and
completely restored in 1965. The house, gallery, and apartments are
furnished with a fine selection of antique furniture. The hotel is the
site of the Library of the Swiss Rose Association, and a permanent
exhibit of watercolors by Lotte Gunthart, a well-known Swiss
painter, is on display.

ADDRESS	Rote Rose
	8158 Regensberg
TELEPHONE	(01) 94.10.13
NUMBER OF ROOMS	2 apartments, each with two rooms and bath
RATES	Apartment with bath and breakfast from 108SF per night
OPEN	Year-round

Motel ST. CHRISTOPHE

An eighteenth-century hotel and restaurant.

ADDRESS	Motel St. Christophe
	1880 Bex
TELEPHONE	(025) 3.67.77
NUMBER OF ROOMS	10 rooms with bath, 5 rooms without bath
RATES	Single room with breakfast (no bath) from 35SF per person per night. Room with bath and breakfast from 45SF per person per night
OPEN	Year-round

Hotel Palazzo SALIS

The Palazzo Salis resembles a miniature French chateau and has been landscaped and furnished in the original style. Built in the sixteenth century as the family residence of the Battista de Salis, it features a Knight's Room on the second floor.

ADDRESS	Hotel Palazzo Salis
	7649 Soglio
TELEPHONE	(082) 4.12.08
NUMBER OF ROOMS	20 rooms without bath
RATES	Single rooms from 35SF to 37SF
OPEN	Mid-November to mid-March

Schlössli SAX

The castle was built in 1551 by Ulrich-Philipp von Sax and in 1615 was sold to the Zurich Cantonal Government. It opened in 1947 as a hotel after being completely renovated.

ADDRESS	Schlössli Sax 9499 Sax
TELEPHONE	(085) 7.12.55
NUMBER OF ROOMS	3 rooms with bath, 7 rooms without bath
RATES	Single room with breakfast from 24SF to 26SF. Room with two meals daily from 41SF to 44SF per person per day
OPEN	Year-round

Hotel-Restaurant SCHLOSS

This castle hotel was the seat of the High Sheriff of St. Gallen Abbey from 1367 to 1798. Built in the early 1600s, it still bears the arms carved in stone of the Abbot Bernhard II Muller. A connecting passage that linked the hotel to a nearby church was destroyed in the eighteenth century. In 1931, the building was completely restored in the original style.

ADDRESS	Hotel-Restaurant Schloss 8590 Romanshorn
TELEPHONE	(071) 63.10.27
NUMBER OF ROOMS	17 rooms without bath, 4 rooms with bath
RATES	Single room with breakfast (no bath) from 27SF to 35SF. Room with bath and breakfast from 33SF to 42SF per night. Room with two meals daily from 47SF to 51SF per person per day
OPEN	Year-round

SCHLOSS-HOTEL

The Schloss-Hotel was built in 1928 on the ruins of the former Palazzo Visconit with dates back to the twelfth century. Enlarged in 1942–44 and again in 1963–65, it features gardens surrounded by ancient walls, subterranean passages, a fifteenth-century tower, and rooms furnished with antiques and paintings.

ADDRESS	Schloss-Hotel 6600 Locarno
TELEPHONE	(093) 31.23.61
NUMBER OF ROOMS	25 rooms with bath, 10 rooms without bath
RATES	Single room with breakfast (no bath) from 35SF to 45SF. Single room with bath and breakfast from 50SF to 70SF per person per night. Room with bath and two meals daily from 62SF to 82SF per person per day
OPEN	Year-round

Hotel SCHWERT

An old alehouse, built between 1620 and 1630, the Schwert was mentioned in local records earlier than Freuler Palace, which is located opposite the hotel. Dining by candlelight is featured in the hotel's restaurant.

ADDRESS	Hotel Schwert 8752 Nafels
TELEPHONE	(058) 34.17.22
NUMBER OF ROOMS	5 rooms with bath, 2 rooms without bath
RATES	Single rooms with bath and breakfast from 65SF to 76SF per person per night. Bathless rooms with breakfast from 32SF to 38SF per night
OPEN	Year-round

Castello del SOLE

The Castello del Sole is a fine old Ticenese house built in the sixteenth-century style and offers spacious rooms, a pergola, loccia, and tavern-bar. On the hotel's grounds are a swimming pool, sauna, solarium, fitness center, and tennis courts.

ADDRESS	Castello del Sole Via Muraccio 6612 Ascona
NUMBER OF ROOMS	49 rooms with bath, 6 rooms without bath
OPEN	April 1 through September

Hotel STADTHAUS BURGDORF

Built in the year 1750 in the Baroque style of architecture, the hotel was originally a town hall and inn.

ADDRESS	Hotel Stadthaus Burgdorf 3400 Burgdorf
TELEPHONE	(034) 22.35.55
NUMBER OF ROOMS	24 rooms with bath or shower
RATES	Single rooms with bath and breakfast from 44SF per person per night
OPEN	Year-round

Hotel STERN

Dating back over three hundred years, the Hotel Stern is located in Chur, along the upper valleys of the Rhine.

ADDRESS	Hotel Stern Reichgasse 11 7000 Chur
TELEPHONE	(081) 22.35.55
TELEX	74198
NUMBER OF ROOMS	46 rooms with bath or shower, five rooms without

RATES	Single rooms from 35SF to 50SF per person per night. Double rooms from 60SF to 86SF per night
OPEN	Year-round
AGENCIES	Romantik Hotels, Relais et Châteaux

Hotel STERN UND POST

The Stern und Post served as a post station along the Gotthard Pass and has been under the ownership of the Tresch family since 1604. The hotel is furnished in period antiques and original paintings, and specializes in regional dishes.

ADDRESS	Hotel Stern und Post 6474 Amsteg
TELEPHONE	(044) 6.44.40
NUMBER OF ROOMS	20 rooms with bath or shower, 22 rooms without
RATES	Single room from 58SF per person per night. Double room from 111SF per night
OWNER-MANAGER	P. A. Tresch
AGENCY	Romantik Hotels

Hotel SWISS CHALET

Four centuries old, this old country house features a gourmet restaurant specializing in regional dishes.

ADDRESS	Hotel Swiss Chalet 6402 Merlischachen
TELEPHONE	(041) 37.12.47
NUMBER OF ROOMS	6 rooms with bath, 14 rooms with or without showers
RATES	Single rooms with bath and breakfast from 60SF to 108SF per person per night. Rooms with bath and three meals daily from 87SF to 164SF per person per day
OPEN	Year-round

Hotel zum TRAUBEN

The Trauben was built in 1648 and is now classified as a national monument. Up until 1798, it was the guest house of the former Lordship of Weinfelden and a meeting place for the annual assembly of the Thurgau Justices. The hotel features old carved-wood ceilings and frescos.

ADDRESS	Hotel zum Trauben 8570 Weinfelden
TELEPHONE	(072) 5.21.41
NUMBER OF ROOMS	8 rooms with bath, 2 rooms without bath
RATES	Single room with bath and breakfast from 32SF to 36SF per person per night
OPEN	Year-round except three weeks in July

Hotel Schlössli VADUZ

The Vaduz, which is actually in Liechtenstein (a small state located between Switzerland and Austria), opened in 1896. An annex, built in the same style, was added in 1974 and consists of apartments decorated and furnished in the Alpine style.

ADDRESS	Hotel Schlössli Vaduz 9490 Vaduz, Liechtenstein
TELEPHONE	(075) 2.11.31
NUMBER OF ROOMS	26 rooms with bath or shower
RATES	Single rooms with bath and breakfast from 72SF to 90SF per person per night. Room with bath and two meals daily from 105SF to 125SF per person per day
OPEN	Year-round

Grand Hotel VICTORIA JUNGFRAU

Built in 1835, the Grand Hotel has been renovated and enlarged several times. The restaurant features gourmet menus and special diet dishes upon request. Former guests include Thomas Edison and Lord Byron.

ADDRESS	Grand Hotel Victoria Jungfrau
	Hoheweg
	3800 Interlaken
TELEPHONE	(036) 21.21.71
NUMBER OF ROOMS	150 rooms with bath, 50 rooms without bath
RATES	Single room with bath and breakfast from 70SF to 150SF. Room with bath and three meals daily from 115SF to 195SF per person per day
OPEN	April 25 to October 15

Le VIEUX MANOIR

ADDRESS	Le Vieux Manoir
	3280 Murten-Meyriez
TELEPHONE	(037) 71.12.83
NUMBER OF ROOMS	12 rooms with bath, 12 rooms without bath
RATES	Single room with breakfast (no bath) from 45SF to 55SF per person per night. Single room with bath and breakfast from 65SF to 80SF per person per night. Room with bath and three meals daily from 135SF to 180SF per person per day
OPEN	March 1 to January 10
AGENCY	Relais et Châteaux

Relais du VIEUX MOULIN

This inn and restaurant is a former millhouse, built in 1840.

ADDRESS	Relais du Vieux Moulin
	1751 Corserey
TELEPHONE	(037) 30.14.44
NUMBER OF ROOMS	15 rooms
OPEN	Year-round

Seehotel WALDSTATTERHOF

The Waldstatterhof opened in the main building in 1870 and was enlarged in 1890. Rebuilt in 1973 and 1974 in the original style, the hotel sits in the middle of a park with a magnificent view of the lakeside. The hotel features the Schoeck Room, named after a well-known Swiss composer, and a large collection of period antiques. The guest log includes the signatures and comments of Queen Vilhelmina of the Netherlands, Winston Churchill, Lian Tun Yen, the Minister of China in 1911, and the Empress Victoria I.

ADDRESS	Seehotel Waldstatterhof
	6440 Brunnen
TELEPHONE	(043) 33.11.33
NUMBER OF ROOMS	108 rooms including self-contained apartments
RATES	Single room with bath and breakfast from 65SF to 105SF. Room with bath and two meals daily from 100SF to 140SF per person per day
OPEN	Year-round

Kurhaus WEISSBAD

The Weissbad spa hotel has existed for four centuries and is now a health resort hotel offering treatment for heart and asthmatic conditions.

ADDRESS	Kurhaus Weissbad
	9057 Weissbad
TELEPHONE	(071) 88.11.61
NUMBER OF ROOMS	11 rooms with bath, 26 rooms without bath
OPEN	April 1 to November 1

Gasthof zum WEISSEN RÖSSLI

Since 1880 this hotel has been owned by its present owners and sits in the hills between the Cantons of Berne and Lucerne. The hotel's restaurant specializes in Emmental dishes.

ADDRESS	Gasthof zum Weissen Rössli
	3532 Zäziwil
TELEPHONE	(031) 91.15.32
NUMBER OF ROOMS	12 rooms without bath
RATES	Single room with breakfast (no bath) from 24SF to 29SF per person per night
OPEN	Year-round
OWNER-MANAGER	The Kunzi Family

WEISSES KREUZ

During the Middle Ages this hotel was the starting point for boat trips to Interlaken, and later became a terminal of the Brunig Railway. The dining room was renovated in 1939 in the original style, and the hotel offers a swimming pool, horse stables, and facilities for water skiing.

ADDRESS	Weisses Kreuz
	3855 Brienz
TELEPHONE	(036) 51.17.81
RATES	Single rooms with bath and breakfast from 35SF to 43SF per person per night
OPEN	Year-round

WEISSES KREUZ

This is the oldest inn in Pontresina, opened in the 1850s with three beds. In 1873, Wilhelm C. Roentgen, famous for his discovery of X-rays, made his first visit to Pontresina, and his name is in the hotel's guest book. Roentgen visited the hotel every year for 43 years, and he became such a favorite guest that one of the hotel's lounge rooms was named after him.

ADDRESS	Weisses Kreuz
	7504 Pontresina
TELEPHONE	(082) 6.63.06
NUMBER OF ROOMS	80 rooms without bath
OPEN	November through April, early June to early October

WEISSES RÖSSLI

The Weisses Rössli is a gabled-roof house located in the old village square of Brunnen. Built around the fifteenth century, it was destroyed by fire, then rebuilt on the same foundation. The Rössli has retained its original style and features wall paintings depicting the hotel's history. Former guests have included Hans Christian Andersen, Queen Victoria, Winston Churchill, and Richard Wagner.

ADDRESS	Weisses Rössli
	6440 Brunnen
TELEPHONE	(043) 31.10.22
NUMBER OF ROOMS	30 rooms
RATES	Single room with bath and breakfast from 36SF to 50SF per person per night. Rooms with bath and three meals daily from 51SF to 75SF per person per day
OPEN	Year-round

Hotel WINKELRIED

Located in a park in the town of Stansstad, the hotel is built around the Schnitzturm, an old tower, built in the twelfth century as a defense against the Hapsburgs.

ADDRESS	Hotel Winkelried
	6362 Stansstad
TELEPHONE	(041) 61.26.22
NUMBER OF ROOMS	20 rooms with bath, 26 rooms without bath
RATES	Year-round

CASTLE HOTEL AGENCIES

Many castle hotels are handled by agencies that solicit business and handle transactions to ease reservations problems. Your travel agent may work directly with these agencies.

We have listed the various castle hotels by agency by country. Several agencies (e.g., Dial Austria) handle castle hotels in one country only. Most, however, seem to represent castle hotels in several countries. And, finally, some of the hotels are represented by more than one agent.

AUSTRIA

Dial Austria handles bookings and reservations and conducts castle-hotel tours customed-designed around the traveler's itinerary. Florentine Helich of Dial Austria offers special rates on tour packages that include room with bath, two meals daily, and use of a rental car. Castle hotels by the Wörthersee are included in a seven six-night tour package that cost 4250AS per person during low season, 5040AS during the high season. A grand tour of Austria lasts eleven days and ten nights and includes stays in some of the finest castle hotels in the country. The cost is 5100AS per person in low season (5895AS in high) and includes room (double occupancy), two meals a day, and assistance in routing along the eight-hundred-mile tour route. For further information, write Florentine Helich, Dial Austria, 3 East 54th Street, New York, NY 10022 (800–221–4980 or, in New York, 838–9677).

Dial Austria Hotels

Hotel Alpha, Vienna
Hotel Burg Bernstein, Bernstein
Hotel Cottage, Salzburg
Schloss-Pension Drasing, Krumpendorf
Hotel Schloss Dürnstein, Dürnstein
Hotel Schloss Ernegg, Steinakirchen am Forst
Schloss Feyregg, Bad Hall
Schloss-Hotel Fondachhof, Salzburg
Hotel de France, Vienna
Hotel Schloss Fuschl, Hof bei Salzburg
Gruenwalderhog, Patsch
Schloss Haunsperg, Oberalm/Hallein
Schlosshotel Igls, Igls
Jormannsdorf, Bad Tatzmannsdorf
Parkhotel Kaernten, Villach
Parkhotel Kummer, Vienna
Schloss Lebenberg, Kitzbühel (Tyrol)
Schloss Leonstain, Pörtschach/Wörthersee
Maria Theresia, Innsbruck
Schloss-Hotel Martinschloss, Klosterneuburg bei Vienna
Gastschloss Mönchstein, Salzburg
Jagdschloss Münichau, Kitzbühel
Norica, Bad Hofgastein
Norica, Maria Alm
Schloss Pichlarn, Irdning
Hotel Prinz Eugen, Vienna
Schloss Rabenstein, Frohnleiten
Graf Recke, Wald im Oberpinzgau
Schloss-Pension St. Martin, St. Martin im Innkreis
Parkhotel Schonbrunn, Vienna
Hotel im Palais Schwarzenberg, Vienna
Schlosshotel Seefeld, Seefeld
Schloss Seefels, Pörtschach/Wörthersee
Schloss Sighartstein, Neumarkt bei Salzburg
Tourotel, Linz
Hotel Schloss Velden, Velden
Hotel Weitzer, Graz
Hotel Winler, Salzburg

Relais et Châteaux (see France)

Arlberg Hospiz, St. Christop
Hotel Bär et Tyrol, Ellmau
Hotel Schloss Dürnstein, Dürnstein
Hotel Schloss Fuschl, Hof bei Salzburg
Gasthof Post, Lech am Arlberg
Hotel im Palais Schwarzenberg, Vienna
Schloss Seefels, Pörtschach/Wörthersee
Hotel Traube, Lienz

Romantik Hotels (see Germany)

Almtalhof, Grunua
Grüner Baum, Badgastein
Modersnof, Weiz
Hotel Musil, Klagenfurt
Hotel Post, Imst/Tirol
Gasthof Post, Lech am Arlberg
Hotel Post, Villach
Graf Recke, Wald im Oberpinzgau
Romischer Kaiser, Vienna
Schlosswirt, Salzburg
Schwarzer Adler, Innsbruck
Tennerhof, Kitzbuhel
Hotel Traube, Lienz
White Horse Inn, St. Wolfgang

Relais du Silence (see France)

Schloss-Hotel Martinschloss, Vienna

Austrian National Tourist Office
545 Fifth Avenue
New York, NY 10017

FRANCE

Relais du Silence is a group of hotels in Europe selected because of their quiet atmosphere, peaceful locations, and personalized service. Many of the hotels are converted castles, chateaux, and palatial estates. Further information is available from Relais du Silence, Hotel Les Oiseaux, Fffl38640, Claix, France.

Relais du Silence Hotels in France

Château d'Agoult, Uze (Gard)
Château de Begue, Cazaubon-Barbotan
Domaine de la Berthelotiere, Nantes
Bon Repos, Montbenoit
Le Bourbail, Pau-Gelos
Le Capitelle, Marmande
Hostellerie du Château, Carpentras (Vancluse)
Château de Chervinges, Villefranche sur Saône (Rhône)
Grand Hôtel Clement, Ardres (Pas-de-Calais)
Château de Collonges, Ruffieux (Savoie)
Donjon de Joy, Sancoins
L' Ecluse, Périgeux
Castle Emeraude, Amélie les Bains (Pyrénées-Orientales)
Hostellerie du Domaine de Fleurac, Fleurac, Jarnac (Charente)
Les Goelands, Royan Pontaillac

Le Grand Hotel, Tence
La Hoirie, Sariat (Dordogne)
La Maronne, Saint-Martin-Valmeroux
Manoir des Ports, Lamballe
Hostellerie Sainte-Catherine, Montbron-Angoulême (Charente)
Château du Scipionnet, Les Vans (Ardèche)
Château des Touches, La Boudranche-Gournay (Deux-Sèvres)
La Tour de Pacoret, Grésy-sur-Isère (Savoie)
Château des Trois Poetes, Castetis-par-Orthez (Pyrénées-Atlantiques)
Château de Violet, Peyriac-Minervois

Relais et Chateaux hotels have varying styles and atmospheres, but most are located in historic buildings and offer excellent facilities. Further information is available from Elizabeth Robinson, Relais et Chateaux, Hotel de Crillon, 10 Place de la Concorde, 75008 Paris, France.

Relais et Chateaux Hotels in France

Hôtel de L'Abbaye, Talloires
Abbaye de Saint Croix, Salon (Provence)
L'Abbaye de Saint-Michel, Tonnerre (Yonne)
Alain Chapel, Mionnay
Domaine d'Auriac, Carcassone (Aude)
Hostellerie du Bas Breau, Barbizon
Chateau du Besset, Romain-de-Lerps
Le Bonne Etape, Chateau-Arnoux
Chateau de Brindos, Anglet
La Residence du Bois, Paris
Le Cabro d'Or, Les Baux de Provence (Bouches-du-Rhône)
Hostelleriè la Cardinale, Baix
Cazaudehore et la Forestière, Saint Germain
Hôtel du Chapon Fin, Thoissey
Domaine de Chateauneuf, Nans-les-Pins
Chateau de la Chevre d'Or, Eze-Village
Hostellerie du Clos, Verneuil-sur-Avre (Eure)
Chateau de Codignat, Lezoux (Puy-de-Dome)
Hostellerie du Chateau de Coudree, Douvaine
Hôtel Crillon, Paris
Hôtel les Frênes, Avignon-Montfavet (Vaucluse)
Bastide Gasconne, Cazaubon (Gers)
Gilvert Laurent, Rive-de-Gier
Hotel Jules César, Arles
Chateau de Larroque, Gimont (Gers)
Hostellerie de Lion d'Or, Liffre
Chateau de Locquenole, Hennebont (Morbihan)
Le Manoir, Fontenay-Tresigny
Chateau de Marcay, Chinon (Indre-et-Loire)
Castel Marie-Louise, La Baule (Morihan)
Mas d'Artigny, St. Paul de Vence

La Mayenelle, Gordes
Le Meaulnes, Nancay (Cher)
Le Mère Blanc, Vonnas
Le Metairie, Mauzac
Le Metropole, Beauileu-sur-Mer
Chalet du Mont d'Arbois, Mont d'Arbois
Chateau de Montledier, Mazamet (Tarn)
Hostellerie du Moulin de l'Abbaye, Brantome-en-Perigord (Dordogne)
Moulin du Roc, Champagnac-de-Belair (Dordogne)
Hostellerie du Moulin de Villeray, Condeau (Ome)
La Musardière, Millau (Aveyron)
Auberge de Noves, Noves (Bouches-du-Rhone)
Hostellerie le Domaine d'Orvault, Orvault
Auberge de Père Bise, Talloires
Domaine de Pèrigny, Les Sorinières
Résidences le Petit Nice Maldorme, Marseille
Chateau de Ponderach, Saint-Pons (Herault)
Hostellerie de la Poste, Avallon (Yonne)
Hostellerie le Prieuré, Avignon
Les Pres d'Eugenie-les-Bains (Landes)
Le Prieure, Gennes (Maine-et-Loire)
Hotel les Prés Fleuris sur Evian, Evian-les-Bains
La Reserve, Pessac Alouette
Hotel Ricordeau, Loue
Chateau de Riell, Molitg-les-Bains (Pyrenees-Orientales)
Chateau de Rochegude, Rochegude (Drome)
Chateau de Roumegouse, Rignac (Aveyron)
Chateau Saint-Martin, Vence
Chateau de Teldras, Cheffes
Auberge des Templiers, Boismorand
Hôtel le Totem, Flaine
Le Bastide de Tourtour, Tourtour
Chateau de Trigance, Trigance (Var)
La Verniaz, Evian-les-Bains
Le Vieux Castillon, Remoulins (Gard)
Le Vieux Logis et ses Logis des Champs, Tremolet

French Government Tourist Office
610 Fifth Avenue
New York, NY 10020

GERMANY

Gast im Schloss is a private organization dedicated to the protection and preservation of historic buildings and hotels in Germany. Representing over one hundred historic hotels, stately manor houses, and inns, Gast im Schloss offers tour packages customdesigned around the traveler's itinerary. The tour includes a special rate for two persons with two meals daily and the use of a rental car. Further information is available from the German National Tourist Office, 630 Fifth Avenue, New York, NY 10020, and Gast im Schloss, Postfach D3526, Trendelberg, West Germany.

Gast im Schloss Hotels

Alte Thorschenke, Cochem-Mosel
Parkhotel Wasserburg Anholt, Anholt (Westfalen)
Schloss Arolsen, Arolsen
Schloss Auel, Lohmar (Wahlscheid)
Schloss Augustenburg, Karlsruhe-Grotzingen
Burghotel Blomberg, Blomberg
Schloss Bothmer, Schwarmstedt-Bothmer
Das Burghaus, Kronenburg/Eifel
Schlosshotel Egg, Egg-Bavarian Forest
Gastehaus Schloss Eggersberg, Riedenburg/Opf.
Hotel Eisenhut, Rothenburg
Waldhotel Friedrichsruhe, b. Ohringen, Württemburg
Fürstenhof, Bad Bruckenau
Schloss Gevelinghausen, Oldsberg
Burghoter Gotzenburg, Jagsthausen
Chateau Gutsch, Luzern
Burg Guttenberg, Neckarmühlbach
Burg Hardenberg, Norten-Harden
Schloss Heinsheim am Neckar, Bad Rappenau-Heinsheim
Schlosshotel auf Burg Hirschhorn, Hirschhorn-Neckar
Schlosshotel Hochhausen, Hassmersheim-Hochhausen
Schloss Hohenfeld, Münster-Roxel
Burg Hornberg, Neckarzimmern
Burghotel Hugenpoet, Essen (Kettwig)
Hotel Kaiserworth, Goslar
Hotel Klostergut Jakobsberg, Boppard/Rhein
Kommende Lage, Rieste
Königliche Villa, Berchtesgaden
Schlosshotel Lembeck, Dorsten (Lembeck)
Park Hotel Maximilian, Begensburg
Hotel Jagdschloss Niederwald, Rüdesheim am Rhein
Schloss Oberstotzingen, Niederstrotzingen
Schloss Petershagen, Petershagen an der WeserHotel Römerkrug, Oberwesel-Rhine
Burghotel Sababurg, Hofgeismar-Sababurg
Der Schafhof, Amorbach-Odenwald
Burghotel Schnellenberg, Attendorn im Sauerland
Burghotel auf Schönburg, Oberwesel am Rhein
Schloss Schonfeld, Kassel
Schlosshotel Burg Schwalenberg, Schieder-Schwalenberg
Hotel Schwan, Bad Karlshafen
Schloss Spangenberg, Spangenburg
Hotel Stadpalais, Lemgo
Hotel Schloss Tremsbüttel, Tremsbüttel (Holstein)
Burg Trendelburg, Trendelburg (Kreis Hofgeismar)

Hotel-Restaurant Schloss Vellberg, Vellberg
Hotel Vorderburg, Schlitz-Hessen
Burg Waldeck, Waldeck am Edersee
Schloss Weitenburg, Kreis Tübingen
Hotel Schloss Wilkenhege, Münster, Westphalia
Burg Windeck, Buhl, Baden
Hotel Burg Winnenthal, Xanten-Winnenthal
Hotel Schloss Zell, Zell/Mosel

Relais et Châteaux (see France)

Alpenhof Murnau, Munich
Le Landhaus Altes Pastorat, Dagebull
Hotel Bad-Schachen, Lindau
Buehlerhoehe, Strasborg
Hotel Eisenhut, Würzburg
Hotel Erbprinz, Baden-Baden
Friedrichsruhe, Stuttgart
Fürstenhof Celle, Celle
Gala im Casino, Bonn
Hotel Geiger, Salzbourg
Stadt Hamburg, Hamburg
Burg Hardenberg, Göttingen
Schloss Hugenpoet, Essen (Kettwigg)
Waldhotel-Kraukramer, Essen
Schlosshotel Kronberg, Kronberg/Taunus
Le Landhaus Leick, Essen
Schlosshotel Monrepos, Stuttgart
Moenches Posthotel, Stuttgart
Le Pflaums Posthotel, Bayreuth
Landhaus Scherrer, Hamburg
Schweizer Stuben, Frankfurt

GERMANY

Romantik Hotels

Adler Post, Titisee-Neustadt
Katzenberger Adler, Rastatt
Alte Post, Wangen
Alte Vogtei, Hamm-Sieg
Zum Alten Brauhaus, Dusseldorf
Altes Brauhaus Burgkeller, Stolberg
Benen-Diken Hof, Keitum
Hotel Bierhüttle, Bierhütte
Clausings Posthotel, Garmisch
Jagdhaus Eiden, Zwichenahn
Haus Elmer, Hamminkeln
Hotel Fasanerie, Zweibrücken
Goldner Lowe, Auerbach
Greifen-Post, Feuchtwangen
Hotel Hahnenkamp, Bad Oeynhausen

Hecht, Überlingen
Zum Heidkrug, Lüneburg
Hotel Hilling, Papenburg
Historischer Krug, Flensburg-Oeversee
Hotel Höttche, Dormagen
Josthof, Salzhausen
Kupferschmiede, Hildesheim
Hof zur Linde, Munster-Handorf
Markustrum, Rothenburg
Meindelei, Bayrischzell
Menzhausen, Uslar
Messerschmitt, Bamberg
Obere Lind, Oberkirch
Zum Oschsen, Kernan-Stetten
Gasthof zur Post, Altötting
Hotel Post, Aschaffenburg
Hotel Post, Nagold
Hotel Post, Wirsberg
Hotel Prinz Carl, Buchen
Ratskeller, Rheda-Wiedenbrück
Zum Ritter, Heidelberg
Hotel Rose, Weissenburg
Hotel Sonne, Badenweiler
Zum Stern, Bad Hersfeld
Stollen, Gutach-Bleibach
Landhaus Stricker, Tinnum
Hotel Strychkaus, Willinger
Hotel Zur Tanne, Braunlage
Waldhorn, Ravensburg
Waldhorn Post, Enzklösterle
Waldschlosschen, Bederkesa
Wehrie, Triberg
Zehntkeller, Iphofen

Relais du Silence (see France)

Goldner Rabe, Furtwangen
Landgasthof Hirsch, Ebnisee
Hotel Muller, Eltmann-Steigerwald
Parkhotel St. Leonhard, Uberlingen
Kurhotel Scheidegg, Scheidegg-Allgaü
Jagdhaus Schwarzer Bok, Buchenberg
Waldhotel der Selighof, Baden-Baden
Waldhotel Standke, Malsch-Waldprechtsweier
Sulzburg, Bad Sulzburg

BTH (see England)

Hotel Drei Lowen, Munich
Etap Haus Berline, Saarbrucken
Etap Kongress Hotel, Saarbrucken
Etap Mainzen Hof, Mainz
Hotel Mondial, Cologne

GREAT BRITAIN

Prestige Hotels represents many of the best personally operated, luxury hotels in Great Britain, and many are located in historic buildings. Some hotels are large, some small, some are modern and some are hundreds of years old. And some offer accommodations in the grand style, while others are geared more toward the homey, historic atmosphere. For further information on Prestige Hotels in Great Britain, write or call Scott Calder International, 295 Madison Avenue, New York, NY 10017 (800–223–5581 or, in New York, 535–9530).

Prestige Hotels in Great Britain

Belfry, Cheshire
Carlton, Bournemouth
The Castle Hotel, Castle Green, Taunton, Somerset
Chewton Glen Hotel, New Milton, Hampshire
The Close at Tetbury, Tetbury, Gloucestershire
Cooden Beach, Sussex
Cottage In The Wood, Worchestershire
Dukes, London
The Elms, Abberley near Worcester
Garden House, Cambridge
Grosvenör, Chester-Cheshire
Hotel Imperial, Hythe, Kent
Inn On the Park, London
The Lygon Arms, Broadway, Worcestershire
Lythe Hill Hotel, Haslemere, Surrey
Marine, South Devon
Meudon, Cornwall
Old Government House, Channel Islands
The Old Swan Hotel, Harrogate, North Yorkshire
Pennyhill Park Hotel, Bagshot, Surrey
Portmeirion, Penrhyndeudraeth
Rookery Hall, Worleston, near Nantwich, Cheshire
Royal, Scarborough
Stafford, London
West Lodge Park Hotel, Hadley Wood, Barnet, Herts
White Hart, Lincolnshire

BTH

BTH operates twenty-nine hotels in England and Scotland. Further information is available from Eric McFerran, BTH, 185 Madison Avenue, New York, NY 10016 (800–221–1074 or, in New York, 684–1820).

BTH in Great Britain

Adelphi Hotel, Liverpool
Charing Cross Hotel, London
Grand Hotel, Hartlepool
Great Eastern Hotel, London
Great Northern Hotel, London
Great Northern Hotel, Peterborough
Great Western Royal Hotel, London
Grosvenor Hotel, London
Manor House Hotel, Moretonhampstead
Midland Hotel, Derby
Midland Hotel, Manchester
Queens Hotel, Leeds
Royal Station Hotel, Hull
Royal Station Hotel, York
Tregenna Castle Hotel, St. Ives, Cornwall
Welcombe Hotel, Stratford-Upon-Avon, Warwickshire

Romantik Hotels in Great Britain (see Germany)

Chedington Court, Chedington, Beaminster, Dorset
Swynford Paddocks, Newmarket, Suffolk
Woodford Bridge Hotel, Holsworthy, Devon, Milton Dameral

Relais et Châteaux Hotels in Great Britain (see France)

Bishoptrow House, Warminster, Wiltshire
Chewton Glen Hotel, New Milton, Hampshire
Gravetye Manor, East Grinstead, West Sussex
Hunstrete House, Chelwood-Bristol
Longueville Manor House, St. Savious, Jersey
Priory House, Bath
Thornbury Castle Restaurant, Thornbury, Bristol

Relais du Silence Hotels in Great Britain

King Harry Hotel, Cornwall

British Tourist Authority
680 Fifth Avenue
New York, NY 10019

IRELAND

The Irish Country House and Restaurant Association represents historic hotels and restaurants throughout Ireland. Further information is available from Jacqueline Morgan, The Irish Country House and Restaurant Association, 10 Heystesbury Street, Dublin 8,

Ireland, or The Irish Tourist Board, 590 Fifth Avenue, New York, NY 10036.

ICHRA Hotels

Ard na Greine Inn, Schull, County Cork
Ardnavha House, County Cork
Assolas Country House, Kanturk, County Cork
Ballinakill House, Waterford
Ballylickey House, County Cork
Ballymaloe House, Shanagarrym, County Cork
Caragh Lodge, County Kerry
Cashel House, Cashel, County Tipperary
Cashel Palace, Cashel, County Tipperary
Crocnaraw House, County Galway
Currarevagh House, County Galway
Gregans Castle, County Clare
The Hunter's Lodge, Rathnew, County Wickow
Inishlounaght House, Marlfield, Clonmel, County Tipperary
Lougueville House, Mallow, County Cork
Marlfield House, Goreu, County Wexford
Mount Falcon Castle, Ballina, County Mayo
Newport House, Newport, County Mayo
The Old Rectory, Wicklow Town, County Wicklow
Rathmullan House, Rathmullan, County Donegal
Roseleague Manor, Letterfrack, County Galway

Relais et Châteaux Hotels (see France)

Cashel House, Cashel, County Tipperary
Newport House, Newport, County Mayo
Rathmullan House, Rathmullan, County Donegal

Irish Tourist Board
590 Fifth Avenue
New York, NY 10036

ITALY

Cigahotels represent many of the best historic hotels in Italy. For further information, contact Cigahotels, Suite 404, 745 Fifth Avenue, New York, NY 10151 (800–221–2340 or, in New York, 935–9540).

Cigahotels in Italy

Duchi d' Aosta, Trieste
Hotel des Bains, Venice-Lido

Des Iles Borromees, Stresa
Cavalieri, Pisa
Hotel Villa Cipriani, Asolo (Trevisa)
Hotel Columbia, Genoa
Hotel Cristallo, Cortina d'Ampezzo
Danieli, Venice
Diana Majestic, Milan
Hotel Europa-Regina, Venice
Hotel Excelsior, Florence
Hotel Excelsior, Naples
Hotel Excelsior, Rome
Hotel Excelsior, Venice-Lido
Palazzo del Giglio, Venice
Le Grand Hotel, Rome
Hotel Palazzo Gritti, Venice
Palace Hotel, Genoa
Park Hotel, Milan
Hotel Principe & Savoia, Milan

Relais et Châteaux Hotels in Italy (see France)

Albergo Splendido, Portofinal
Hotel Certosa di Maggiono, Siena
Hotel Cipriani, Venice
Hotel Villa Cipriani, Asolo (Treviso)
Hotel Domink, Brixen-Sudtirol
Villa d'Este, Cernobbio
Hotel Castel Freiberg, Merano (Bolzano)
Gallia Palace Hotel, Punt Ala
Gualtiero Marchesi, Milan
Grand Hotel Villa Igiea, Palermo (Sicily)
Hotel Lord Byron, Rome
La Meridiana, Garlenda
Il Morus, Sta. Margherita
Pavillion, Courmayeur
Il Pellicano, Porto Erocle
Hotel Pitrizza, Port Cervo
Villa la Principessa, Massa Pisana, Lucca
Le Regency, Florence
Rio Envers Fallia, San Sicaro
Hotel Palazzo San Domenico, Taormina (Sicily)
Villa Sassi, Torino
Sporting Rotondo, Port Rotondo
Tre Vaselle, Torginao

Romantik Hotels in Italy (see Germany)

Hotel Turm

BTH in Italy (see Great Britain)

Etap Astoria, Florence
Etap Bologna, Bologna
Etap Boston, Rome
Parkhotel, Venice

Italian Government Travel Office
630 Fifth Avenue
New York, NY 10020

SPAIN

The Secretariat of State for Tourism in Spain operates a network of unique, historic hotels called *paradors* and mountain shelters known as *refugios de Montana*. Most are located in historic cities or in the Spanish countryside and consist of old castles, monasteries, abbeys, convents, and palaces that have been renovated and modernized to serve as comfortable hotels. Paradors offer rooms with baths, elegant dining, and a full complement of services. Refugios are often located in the remote corners of Spain, away from the tourist crowds. Not as elegant as paradors, they are an excellent choice for travelers interested in getting-away-from-it-all, fishing, hunting, and walking tours of nearby villages.

Further information is available from the Spanish National Tourist Office, 665 Fifth Avenue, New York, NY 10022 (212–859–8822).

Spanish Paradors

Del Adelantado, Cazorla
Del Alabarino, Cambados
Parador Nacional Alcazar del Rey Don Pedro, Camona (Sevilla)
Del Almagro, Almagro
De Antequera, Antiquera
Antonio Machado, Soria
Aran, Viella
Parador de Argomaniz, Argomaniz (Alava)
La Arruzafa, Cordoba
Altantico, Cadiz
De Bailen, Bailen
Parador Casa del Baron, Pontevedra
Del Bierzo, Villafranca del Bierzo
La Canadas del Teide, Canadas del Teide
Parador Nacional Carlos V, Jarandilla de la Vera (Cáceres)
Del Comendador, Cáceres
Parador La Concordia, Alcaniz (Teruel)

Parador Nacional Conde de Gondomar, Bayona (Pontevedra)
Conde de la Gomera, San Sebastian de la Gomera
Parador Nacional Conde de Orgaz, Toledo
Parador Condestable Davalos, Ubeda (Jaén)
Parador de los Condes de Alba y Aliste, Zamora
Parador Condes de Villalba, Villalba
Casa del Corregidor, Argos de la Frontera
Costa Blanca, Javea
Costa Brava, Aiguablava-Bagur
Costa de la Luz, Ayamonte
Costa del Azahar, Benicarlo
Cristobal Colon, Mazagon
De Cruz de Tejeda, Cruz de Tejeda
Parador Nacional Duques de Cardona, Cardona (Barcelona)
Del El Ferrol, El Ferrol
Parador El Emperador, Fuenterrabia (Guipuzcoa)
Parador Enrique II, Ciudad Rodrigo (Salamanca)
Del Estudiante, Alcala de Henares (Madrid)
Parador Rey Fernando II de Leon, Benavente (Zamora)
Fuentes Carrionas, Cervera de Pisuerga
De Fuerteventura, Fuerteventura
Don Gaspar de Portola, Arties
Gibralfaro, Malaga
Parador Nacional Gil Blas, Santillana del Mar (Santander)
Del Golf, Torremolinos
De Gredos, Gredos-Navarredonda
Parador Hernan Cortez, Zafra (Badajoz)
Hierro, El Hierro
Luis Vives, El Saler
La Mancha, Albacete
De Manzanares, Manzanares
De Marco Fabio Quintiliano, Calahorra
Parador del Marques de Villena, Alacon
Molino Viejo, Gijon
Monte Perdido, Bielsa
Parador Nacional de Monterrey, Verin (Orense)
Don Pedro de Estopiana, Melilla
De Puebla de Sanabria, Puebla de Sanabria
Parador Puerto de Pajares, Pajares
De Puerto Lumbreras, Puerto Lumbreras
De Puertomarin, Puertomarin
Parador Raimundo de Borgona, Avila
Rednando de Aragon, Sos del Rey Catolico
Hotel de los Reyes Católicos, Santiago de Compostela (La Coruña)
De Ribadeo, Ribadeo
Salamanca, Salamanca
Parador Nacional San Francisco, Alhambra (Granada)
San Telmo, Tuy
Parador Nacional Castillo de Santa Catalina, Jaén
Santa Cruz de la Palma, Santa Cruz de la Palma

Parador Santo Domingo de la Calzada, Santo Domingo (Logrono)
Seo de Urgel, Seo de Urgel
Segovia, Segovia
Sierra Nevada, Sierra Nevada-Monachil
Parador Nacional Castillo de Siguenza, Siguenza (Guadalajara)
Teruel, Teruel
Tordesillas, Tordesillas
Parador Nacional Via de la Plata, Merida (Badajoz)
Parador Principe de Viana, Olite (Navarra)
Villacastin, Villacastin
Parador Virrey Toledo, Oropesa (Toledo)
Parador Castillo de la Zuda, Tortosa (Tarragona)
Parador Nacional de Zurbana, Guadalupe (Cáceres)

Entursa is a hotel management company associated with the Spanish National Tourist Office and operates and maintains ten deluxe historic hotels across Spain. Since its founding in 1954, Entursa has spent over $35 million in restoring these landmark buildings. Don Salvador Fernandez, president of Entursa, considers his group to be the major custodians of Spain's priceless native heritage. In restoring these buildings, local artisans are chosen specifically to fashion something as simple as a door handle. Fifteen different experts in the fields of rugmaking, woodwork, and historic restoration are employed by Entursa.

Entursa schedules packaged tours of these famous hotels that include accommodations, meals, and use of a rental car. An eight-day package with room costs about $212 per person, double occupancy (airfare not included). Use of a rental car for eight days boosts this tour package to $275 per person during the low season (November 1 to December 31) and $313 per person during the high season (April 1 to October 30).

This tour begins in Madrid with accommodations at the Charmartin Hotel, then proceeds to the Santa Maria de la Paular Hotel in Rascafría, the San Marcos Hotel in León, the Los Reyes Católicos Hotel in Santiago de Compostela and back to Madrid.

Further information is available from Reservation Systems, Inc., 6 East 46th Street, New York, NY 10017 (800–223–1588 or, in New York 661–4540).

Entursa Hotels

Hotel Alfonso XIII, Sevilla
Chamartin, Madrid
Jerez, Jerez de la Frontera
Mencey, Santa Cruz de Tenerife
Hotel la Muralla, Ceuta
Hotel de los Reyes Católicos, Santiago de Compostela (La Coruña)
Hotel San Marcos, León

Hotel Santa Maria el Paular, Rascafría (Madrid)
Sarria, Barcelona

Relais et Châteaux (see France)
Hostal de la Gavina, S'Agaro
Grand Hotel la Toja, La Toja
Hotel Hacienda, San Miguel Ibiza
Juan Arzac, San Sebastian
Landa Palace, Burgos
Marbella, Marbella
Monte Picayo, Valencia-Puzol
Los Monteros, Marbella
El Montiboli, Villajovosa
Hotel Santa Marta, Lloret de Mar
Hotel Son Vida, Palma de Mallorca
Zalacain, Madrid

BTH (see Great Britain)
Etap Calatrava Hotel, Madrid

Spanish National Tourist Office
665 Fifth Avenue
New York, NY 10022

SWITZERLAND

Relais du Silence Hotels in Switzerland (see France)
Parkhotel Adler, Fribourg
Le Mont Blanc, Plan Mayens-Crans
Ratia Hotel, Klosters Dorf
Hotel Residence, Grindelwald
Hotel Residence, Wengen
Parkhotel Wehle, Fribourg
Hotel Zayette, Leukerbad

Romantik Hotels in Switzerland (see Germany)
Chesa Griseun, Klosters
Hotel Guardaval, Bad Scoul-Tarasp
Hotel Krone, Dietikon
Hotel Krone, Gottlieben
Hotel Santis, Appenzell
Hotel Stern, Chur
Hotel Stern und Post, Amsteg
Sternen, Kriegstetten
Hotel Ticino, Lugano
Hotel Wilden Mann, Lucerne

Relais et Châteaux Hotels in Switzerland (see France)

Alpenrose, Schonried
Hostellerie des Chevalier, Gruyeres
Le Coq d'Or, Locarno
Le Grappe d'Or, Lausanne
Guarda Val Sporz, Lenzerheide
Hotel Stern Und Post, Amsteg
Stucki, Bale
Hotel Victoria, Glion
Le Vieux Manoir, Murten-Meyriez
Waldhaus Hotel, Horw Luzern

Swiss National Tourist Office
605 Fifth Avenue
New York, NY 10020

GLOSSARY

ABBEY
   a monastery or a church connected with a monastery
ABBOT
   the superior or governor of an abbey or monastery
ARBORETUM
   from *arbor*; a place with trees
ARCHBISHOP
   a chief bishop who presides over an archbishopric or arch-
   diocese
BARONIAL
   pertaining to a baron, his estate or class; originally, barons
   were the proprietors of land held by honorable service and in
   ancient records, the word *baron* was used to identify any
   nobility
BAROQUE
   of or characteristic of art and architecture featuring ornamenta-
   tion and curved rather than straight lines; overdecorated; from
   the period 1500–1750
BAVARIA
   an area in southwestern Germany; the largest state in the
   Federal Republic of Germany
BENEDICTINE
   a monk or nun of the Benedictine monastery, founded in 529
   A.D.
CANTABRIAN
   an area in Spain
CANTON
   one of the political divisions of a country or territory; in
   Switzerland, a state; in France, a subdivision containing a
   group of communes; in architecture, a corner or pilaster of any
   projection

CAPITAL
> the head or upmost member of any part of a building; the uppermost part of a column, pillar, or pilaster, serving as the head or crowning and placed over the shaft

CASTILE
> pertaining to Castile, Spain, and its people; an area in Spain well-known for its castles and historic buildings

CISTERCIAN
> from the Latin *cistercium* or French *citeaux*; the original convent

CISTERCIAN ORDER
> monastic order, branch of the Benedictine Order, established in Citeaux, France, in 1098

CLOISTERS
> a monastery or nunnery; a house inhabited by monks or nuns; in architecture, an arcade or colonnade, a covered walk along the walls of a port of ecclesiastical or monastic buildings

COLONNADE
> a series of columns; in architecture, any series or range of columns placed at certain intervals

CUPOLA
> in architecture, a small dome or similar structure on the roof

ELIZABETHAN
> of or characteristic of the time when Elizabeth I was Queen of England

FRANCISCAN
> designating or of the Roman Catholic Order of St. Francis, formed in Italy in 1209 by St. Francis of Assisi

FRIEZE
> a decoration or series of decorations forming an ornamental band around a room; in architecture, a horizontal band, usually decorated with sculpture, between the cornices of a building

GALICIAN
> a native or inhabitant of Spanish Galicia on the northern coast of Spain

GEORGIAN
> of the reigns of George I, II, III, and IV of England from 1740–1830; designating an architectural style of these periods

GOTHIC
> of a style of architecture developed in western Europe between the twelfth and sixteenth centuries; characterized by the use of ribbed vaulting, flying buttresses, pointed arches, and steep roofs

HANSEATIC
> a medieval league of free towns in northern Germany and adjoining countries, formed for the economic advancement and protection of residents; of the Hanse or the towns that formed it

HUGUENOTS
    any French Protestant of the sixteenth and seventeenth
    centuries; a sworn companion or confederate influenced by
    Besançon Hugues, a Geneva reformer
IONIC
    designating a Greek style of architecture characterized by
    ornamental scrolls on the capitals; one of the three Greek
    architectural styles, distinguished by the volute of its capital
JACOBEAN
    of the period of James 1, 1603–25
JACOBITE
    a partisan or adherent of James II, King of England; one of a
    sect of Christians in Styria and Mesopotamia, named after
    Jacob Baradzi, a sixth-century leader
LOGGIA
    an arcaded roof gallery built into or projecting from the side of
    a building, particularly one overlooking an open court
MEDIEVAL
    belonging to the Middle Ages, 500 A.D.–1450 A.D.
MESOPOTAMIAN
    designating or belonging to Mespotamia, an ancient country
    lying between the rivers Euphrates and Tigris
MOORISH
    a style of architecture used by the Moors of Spain and North
    Africans in mosques and public places; also called Sacancenic
    or Arabian architecture. It is distinguished by the prevailing
    use of the arch in a horseshoe shape; lofty, elongated cupolas
    and elaborate surface decoration; interior surfaces are covered
    with richly-colored arabesques and geometrical designs
MOSQUE
    a temple or place of adoration
NASSAU
    a health resort area in Germany, near the Lahn River
NECROPOLIS
    a cemetery belonging to a city
NORMAN
    any of the Northmen who occupied Normandy in the tenth
    century; designating or of the Romanesque style of architecture
    as it flourished in Normandy after the Norman conquest in
    1066, characterized by massive construction, round arches over
    recessed doors and elaborate carvings
PALLADIAN
    in ancient Greece and Rome, any statue of the Greek goddess,
    Pallas Athena; any safeguard as of a city or institution
PARAPETS
    walls or banks used to screen troops from frontal attacks;
    something placed along the top of a rampart; a wall or railing
    to protect people from falling on a balcony or ridge

PILASTERS
> rectangular supports or piers treated architecturally as a
> column with a base, shaft, and capital

PROVENCE
> an area in southern France; the medieval language of southern
> France as cultivated by troubadours; one of Europe's great
> literary languages, based on the Romance languages

PYRENEES
> a mountain range between France and Spain

RAMPART
> an embankment of earth surmounted by a parapet and
> encircling a castle or fortress for defense against attack

REGENCY
> in England, the period between 1811 and 1820; in France,
> between 1715 and 1723; characterized in art by scrollwork
> combined with natural forms, many curves and strict balance
> proportion; a designation or of a style of furniture developed
> in France between 1715 and 1723

ROMANESQUE
> designating or of a style of European architecture of the
> eleventh and twelfth centuries; based on the Roman and
> characterized by the use of a round arch and wall, thick walls
> and interior bays

SARACEN
> originally any member of the Nomadic tribes of Syria and its
> nearby regions; anyone opposed to the Crusaders

SPANDRELS
> in architecture, the triangular space between the outer curve of
> an arch and the rectangular frame or enclosure; one of the
> spaces between a series of arches and a cornice running above
> them

SPRINGER
> the point at which an arch unites with its support; the bottom
> stone of an arch or the rib of a groined roof

TYROL
> a region in the Alps between western Austria and northern
> Italy

VENETIAN
> a style of Italian architecture developed by Venetian architects
> from the twelfth century to the early part of the sixteenth
> century—typically, each story is provided with its own tier of
> columns or pilasters with their entablature and separated from
> other stories by conspicuous friezes or belts, often in the form
> of balustrades broken up by columns and pedestals decorated
> with figurines, and the arched windows are ornamental and
> often filled with figurines; the color is rich, characterized by
> ornate, flowery carvings, and the use of marble and mosaics

VICTORIAN
> of or characteristic of the time when Victoria was Queen of England from 1837 to 1901; a style of architecture and furniture

VISIGOTHIC
> of or characteristic of any of the West Goths, a Teutonic people who invaded the Roman Empire late in the 4th century and set up a kingdom in France and Spain which lasted until 700 A.D.

VOLUTE
> a spiral scroll forming one of the main features of Ionic and Corinthian capitals

WESTFALIA (WESTPHALIA)
> an area in western Germany where the Roman Leagues of Varus met their defeat, thereby stopping the conquest of Germany

The Great European Castle Hotel Tour

The decision to invite a select group of travelers to join us on our next European castle-hunting expedition was made when we discovered the interest in Europe's historic hotels and the lack of personalized, special-interest trips of this kind. These tours will take us on 14–30 day trips into the heart of France, Switzerland, Spain, Austria, Germany, Italy, and across the United Kingdom as we search for these yet-to-be-discovered special places. The itinerary will vary with each trip, based on the interests of participants and what our research uncovers. Some of the hotels listed in this guide will be included and a special trip into Eastern Europe is being planned. The tour will consist of roundtrip airfare, all ground transportation, accommodations and meals and sightseeing trips upon arrival. Tour costs will be based on the type of accommodations and meals provided, but you can be assured they'll all fall into the *luxurious* range. If you're interested in joining one of our upcoming research tours, you can contact us at 5305 Northwest 57th Lane, Gainesville, Florida 32606.

About the Authors

Phil Philcox and Beverly Boe are a husband-wife team who have traveled around the world looking for special vacationing experiences to write about. While living in France between 1963–1966, they discovered their first historic hotel, a 16th-century Swiss chateau tucked in the Alps' foothills between France and Italy and since then, they've traveled tens of thousands of road miles through England, Scotland, Wales, France, Belgium, Germany, Austria, Switzerland, Italy, Yugoslavia, Spain, and Poland compiling material and photographing these historic places.

As freelance writers-photographers and editors of The Press Association of Florida, their articles have appeared in *Travel-Holiday, Travel, World Traveler, Consumer's Digest, Playboy* and over five hundred magazines worldwide, including magazines in France, England, Germany, and Australia.

Their syndicated travel column, "The Smart Traveler," appears monthly in magazines reaching over three million readers, and they're the authors of seven travel guides, including *The Tampa Guide: An Adventurer's Guide To Europe* (Motorbooks International), *The Smart Traveler's Information Almanac* (East Wood Press), and *Europe...The Two-Wheeled Adventure* (Chateau).

Phil Philcox is the former travel editor of the Overseas News Media of New York and European correspondent for *Skin Diver* magazine. Beverly Boe holds a master's degree in Human and Behavioral Sciences from the University of South Florida. They live in Gainesville, Florida.